Enchantment

Also by Guy Kawasaki

The Art of the Start

Rules for Revolutionaries

The Macintosh Way

Selling the Dream

How to Drive Your Competition Crazy

Hindsights

The Computer Curmudgeon

Database 101

Reality Check

Guy Kawasaki

Enchantment

The Art of Changing Hearts, Minds, and Actions

Portfolio/Penguin

PORTFOLIO / PENGUIN
Published by the Penguin Group
Penguin Group (USA) Inc., 375 Hudson Street, New York, New York 10014, U.S.A. • Penguin Group (Canada), 90 Eglinton Avenue East, Suite 700, Toronto, Ontario, Canada M4P 2Y3 (a division of Pearson Penguin Canada Inc.) • Penguin Books Ltd, 80 Strand, London WC2R 0RL, England • Penguin Ireland, 25 St. Stephen's Green, Dublin 2, Ireland (a division of Penguin Books Ltd) • Penguin Books Australia Ltd, 250 Camberwell Road, Camberwell, Victoria 3124, Australia (a division of Pearson Australia Group Pty Ltd) • Penguin Books India Pvt Ltd, 11 Community Centre, Panchsheel Park, New Delhi—110 017, India • Penguin Group (NZ), 67 Apollo Drive, Rosedale, Auckland 0632, New Zealand (a division of Pearson New Zealand Ltd) • Penguin Books (South Africa) (Pty) Ltd, 24 Sturdee Avenue, Rosebank, Johannesburg 2196, South Africa

Penguin Books Ltd, Registered Offices:
80 Strand, London WC2R 0RL, England

First published in 2011 by Portfolio / Penguin,
a member of Penguin Group (USA) Inc.

10   9   8   7   6   5   4   3

Copyright © Guy Kawasaki, 2011
All rights reserved

Illustration credits
Page xxi: Used by permission of Apple; 7: By Jorge Cham (www.phdcomics.com); 8: Courtesy of Eric Dawson; 16, 18, 43, 58, 65, 102, 117, 118 (both photographs), 119 (both), 120 (both), 121, 192 (top left), 196: Courtesy of the author; 25: Courtesy of Fran Shea; 37: Courtesy of Tony Morgan; 45: Provided by Korey Kay & Partners Advertising, New York; 53: Courtesy of Mike Stevens; 68 (top): © Derek Sivers (www.sivers.org); 68 (bottom): Courtesy of Matt Maurer; 78: Rob McCullough; 93: Courtesy of Richard Fawal; 111: Courtesy of Chris Anthony; 133 (bottom): Courtesy of Garr Reynolds; 146: Provided by Visible Measures (www.visiblemeasures.com); 150: Courtesy of Meryl K. Evans; 158: Gray Rinehart; 163: Courtesy of Milene Laube Dutra; 171: Courtesy of David Stockwell; 182: Courtesy of Tibor Kruska; 184: Courtesy of Kathy Parsanko; 192 (bottom left): By Samuel Toh; 193 (top): By Tracy Lucas of Four Square Creative Services; 194: Courtesy of Ade Harnusa Azril; 195: Sarah Adams; Certain credits appear adjacent to the respective images.

Library of Congress Cataloging-in-Publication Data
Kawasaki, Guy, 1954–
Enchantment : the art of changing hearts, minds, and actions / Guy Kawasaki.
p.   cm.
Includes bibliographical references and index.
ISBN 978-1-59184-379-5
1. Persuasion (Psychology) in organizations. 2. Persuasion (Psychology) 3. Influence (Psychology) 4. Marketing—Psychological aspects. 5. Management—Psychological aspects. I. Title.
HD30.3.K38 2011
658.8001'9—dc22   2010046009

Printed in the United States of America
Interior and case design including butterfly illustration by Daniel Lagin
Butterfly photograph by Sarah Brody • Butterfly created by Michael LaFosse

Many men can make a fortune but very few can build a family.

—**J. S. Bryan**

To my wife, Beth, and my four children, Nic, Noah, Nohemi, and Nate . . . because they enchant me every day.

Acknowledgments

Gratitude unlocks the fullness of life. It turns what
we have into enough, and more. It turns denial into
acceptance, chaos to order, confusion to clarity. It can
turn a meal into a feast, a house into a home, a
stranger into a friend.

—Melody Beattie (author of *Codependent No More*)

Publishing a book is not a solitary effort. Yes, an author must open a
vein and let the words pour out, but publishing is a long process from
plasma to pages. Close to one hundred people helped me finish this
book, and I'd like to acknowledge their efforts.

Indispensables: My wife, Beth Kawasaki, and my best friend,
Will Mayall.

Early architects: Marylene Delbourg-Delphis and Bill Meade.

Beyond the call of duty: Sarah Brody, Taly Weiss, Jon Winokur,
Anne Haapanen, Kate Haney, Tina Seelig, Steve Martin,
and Bruna Martinuzzi.

Contributors: Mari Smith and Greg Jarboe.

Penguin: The ever patient Rick Kot, Joe Perez, Kyle Davis, Jacquelynn Burke, Allison "Sweetness" McLean, Laura Tisdel, Gary Stimeling, Will Weisser, and Adrian Zackheim.

Muscle: Sloan Harris.

Research: Catherine Faas.

Beta testers: Karen Lai, Jennifer Jones, Alison van Diggelen, Ed Morita, Alfonso Guerra, Jim Simon, Cerise Welter, Brad Hutchings, Scott Yoshinaga, Gary Pinelli, Web Barr, Terri Lowe, Dan Agnew, Terri Mayall, Gary Pinelli, Harish Tejwani, Bill Lennan, Kelsey Hagglund, Lisa Nirelli, Matt Maurer, Tammy Cravit, Tariq Ahmad, Kip Knight, Geoff Baum, Milene Laube Dutra, Brent Kobayashi, Alex de Soto, Patricia Santhuff, Daniel Pellarini, Mitch Grisham, Stevie Goodson, Fernando Garcia, Ken Graham, Steve Asvitt, Charlotte Sturtz, Kelly Haskins, Lindsay Brechler, Shoshana Loeb, Halley Suitt, Barbara French, Zarik Boghossian, Imran Anwar, Ravit Lichtenberg, and Matt Kelly.

Cover: Sarah Brody, Ade Harnusa Azril, Michael G. LaFosse, Richard Alexander, Lisa Mullinaux, Ross Kimbarovsky (and the Crowdspring crew), Jason Wehmhoener, Jean Okimoto, Gina Poss, and Marco Carbullido.

PowerPoint: Ana Frazao.

Marketing: Catri Velleman, Allen Kay, and Neenz Faleafine.

Restaurant: La Tartine in Redwood City, California.

Music: Pandora's Adult Contemporary channel.

Leaving out anyone who helped is a most unenchanting act, so I apologize in advance if I did this. Let me know at Guy@alltop.com, and I'll get this fixed in future printings.

Anyway, here's my big "Mahalo" to you all. I could not have done this without you.

Contents

Buying books would be a good thing if one could
also buy the time to read them in; but as a rule the
purchase of books is mistaken for the appropriation
of their contents.

—Arthur Schopenhauer

Chapter 5: How to Launch   55

Chapter 6: How to Overcome Resistance   70

Chapter 10: How to Enchant Your Employees   151

Chapter 11: How to Enchant Your Boss   165

Introduction

> The difficulty lies, not in the new ideas, but in
> escaping from the old ones, which ramify, for those
> brought up as most of us have been, into every
> corner of our minds.
>
> —**John Maynard Keynes**

My Story

I first saw a Macintosh in the summer of 1983, six months before the rest of the world. Mike Boich showed it to me in the back of a one-story office building on Bandley Drive in Cupertino, California. At the time, Boich was the software evangelist for the Macintosh Division of Apple. I was a humble jeweler, schlepping gold and diamonds for a small jewelry manufacturer out of Los Angeles. Macintosh was a rumor. And the only reason I saw it so early was that Boich was my college roommate.

Back then, "personal computing" was an oxymoron because Fortune 500 companies, universities, and governments owned most computers. If you were lucky, you owned an Apple IIe or an IBM PC. They displayed upper- and lower-case text, and you navigated around

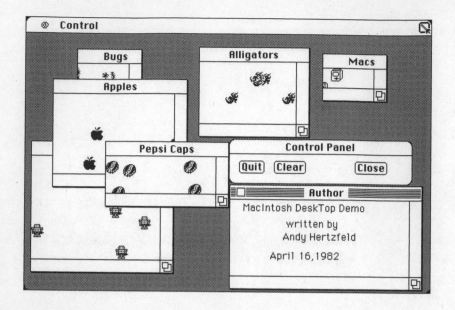

the screen with cursor keys. Most of the world used IBM Selectric typewriters, and the lucky people had access to the model with the lift-off correcting tape.

Seeing a Macintosh for the first time was the second most enchanting moment of my life (the first most enchanting moment was meeting my wife). My introduction to Macintosh removed the scales from my eyes, parted the clouds, and made me hear angels singing.

Let's go back in time to see two features that made the Macintosh so cool. First, it could display animated graphics. Andy Hertzfeld, the Macintosh Division's "software wizard," created a program with bouncing Pepsi caps to show off this capability. Steve Jobs then used Andy's program to convince John Sculley, CEO of Pepsi, to "stop selling sugared water" and join Apple. This application seems simple now, but back then bouncing icons inside windows was magic.

Second, with a Macintosh program called MacPaint, people could draw pictures such as this woodcut geisha by Susan Kare, the division's

graphic artist. When Boich showed me what MacPaint could do, my mind did somersaults. Back then, the most people could do on a personal computer was hack out crude pictures using letters and numbers. With a Macintosh, anyone could at least draw diagrams, if not create art.

A few minutes of Boich's demo convinced me of two things: First, the Macintosh would make people more creative and productive than they'd ever dreamed; and second, I wanted to work for Apple. Boich got me a job in the Macintosh Division, and my mission was to convince developers to create Macintosh-compatible products. I used fervor and zeal to make them believe in the Macintosh as much as I did.

This job marked the beginning of a twenty-five-year fascination with the art of enchantment. I define *enchantment* as the process of delighting people with a product, service, organization, or idea. The outcome of enchantment is voluntary and long-lasting support that is mutually beneficial.

Our Journey

This book is for people who see life for what it *can* be rather than what it can't. They are bringing to market a cause—that is, a product, service, organization, or idea—that can make the world a better place. They realize that in a world of mass media, social media, and advertising media, it takes more than instant, shallow, and temporary relationships to get the job done.

I am going to take you on a journey to learn how to change the hearts, minds, and actions of people. Here is our itinerary:

CHAPTER 1: WHY ENCHANTMENT?

The greater your goals, the more you'll need to change people's hearts, minds, and actions. This is especially true if you have few resources and big competitors. If you need to enchant people, you're doing something meaningful. If you're doing something meaningful, you need enchantment.

CHAPTER 2: HOW TO ACHIEVE LIKABILITY

Has anyone you disliked ever enchanted you? I doubt it. If he* did, I doubt the feeling lasted long. This is why the first step of enchantment is to get people to like you. To accomplish this, you'll need to accept others and find something to like in them.

CHAPTER 3: HOW TO ACHIEVE TRUSTWORTHINESS

Has anyone you distrusted ever enchanted you? I doubt this, too. Achieving trustworthiness is the second step. People trust you when you are knowledgeable, competent, make bigger pies, and create

---

* This is the first instance where I could pick a masculine (he) or feminine (she) pronoun, use a plural pronoun (they), or the ever-awkward composite (he/she). In general, I use *she* when the person is a positive example. This is my small effort to counteract the short-changing of women in literature for thousands of years.

win-win situations—in short, when you do the right things the right way.

CHAPTER 4: HOW TO PREPARE

Great products, services, organizations, and ideas are enchanting. Crap is not. Preparing to enchant people requires creating something great, communicating it in short, simple, and swallowable terms, and working your butt off to get it to market before your competition.

CHAPTER 5: HOW TO LAUNCH

Great enchanters ship. This is what Richard Branson and Steve Jobs do better than anyone else. Ever. Launching your cause involves immersing people in your cause, getting them to at least try it, and recruiting your first followers to help you spread the word.

CHAPTER 6: HOW TO OVERCOME RESISTANCE

People often accept "good enough" products and services because they are busy or don't know better. You will encounter resistance to change in these situations. The way to overcome resistance is to provide social proof, find a way to agree, and enchant all the influencers.

CHAPTER 7: HOW TO MAKE ENCHANTMENT ENDURE

Enchantment is a process, not an event. You want your efforts to endure, and this requires that people internalize your cause, reciprocate, and fulfill their commitments. It also helps to build an ecosystem of resellers, consultants, developers, and user groups around your cause.

CHAPTER 8: HOW TO USE PUSH TECHNOLOGY

Have you wondered how to use PowerPoint, Twitter, and e-mail to push out information? These products can enable you to bring your story to the people you want to enchant. This chapter explains how to do this using the latest technology.

CHAPTER 9: HOW TO USE PULL TECHNOLOGY

In addition to push technology, there's pull technology. In this case, you bring people to your story instead of bringing your story to people. This chapter focuses on using Web sites, blogs, Facebook, LinkedIn, and YouTube to enchant people and encourage them to come to you.

CHAPTER 10: HOW TO ENCHANT YOUR EMPLOYEES

Enchantment is not only an outbound activity, but one that you should direct at your employees, too. If you provide them with the opportunity to master skills, the autonomy to work independently, and the chance to realize a positive purpose, you can enchant your employees.

CHAPTER 11: HOW TO ENCHANT YOUR BOSS

Imagine working for someone you've enchanted. The benefits include freedom, flexibility, money, and mentoring. Enchanting your boss requires reprioritizing your efforts to make her successful—but the outcome is worth it.

CHAPTER 12: HOW TO RESIST ENCHANTMENT

Not every enchanting person has your best interests at heart. Resisting enchantment, therefore, is a valuable skill that requires avoiding tempting situations, looking far into the future, and finding a devil's advocate. After reading this chapter, you may even be able to resist Apple's products.

Let's Get Started

By reading this book, you will learn how to apply my experiences as an evangelist, entrepreneur, and venture capitalist to make your "Macintosh" successful. I'm passing my knowledge on so you can change the world. There is no greater reward for an author than to see how people use his work, so I'm anxious to get started.

Guy Kawasaki
Silicon Valley, California
2011

Enchantment

Chapter 1
Why Enchantment?

You have first to experience what you want to express.

—Vincent van Gogh

The world will not beat a path to your door for an insanely great mousetrap. In fact, the greater the mousetrap, the more difficult it is to get people to embrace it because it is so different from what people are used to. This chapter explains what enchantment is, when and why you need it, and the ethics of enchanting people.

What Is Enchantment?

When Karin Muller, filmmaker and author, was in the Peace Corps from 1987 to 1989, she dug wells and built schools in a village in the Philippines. One night, seventeen members of the New People's Army (NPA), the armed wing of the Communist Party of the Philippines, came to her hut to interrogate her. Earlier that day, villagers had warned her that this was going to happen, so she collected two precious commodities: sugar and coffee.

When the NPA arrived, she exclaimed, "Thank God you're here. I've been waiting all day. Please have some coffee. Leave your guns at the door." Her reaction baffled the leader of the group, but he took off his gun and sat down for a cup of coffee. She avoided an interrogation or something worse because, according to Muller, "You can't interrogate someone you're having coffee with."

Muller did not react with anger, indignation, or panic (which is how I would have reacted). Instead, she touched an emotion in the leader of the group and transformed the situation from brute force and intimidation to conversation and communication. She delighted him with her unexpected hospitality and changed his heart, his mind, and his actions.

In short, she enchanted him.

Enchantment can occur in villages, stores, dealerships, offices, boardrooms, and on the Internet. It causes a voluntary change of hearts and minds and therefore actions. It is more than manipulating people to help you get your way. Enchantment transforms situations and relationships. It converts hostility into civility. It reshapes civility into affinity. It changes skeptics and cynics into believers.

When Is Enchantment Necessary?

There are many tried-and-true methods to make a buck, yuan, euro, yen, rupee, peso, or drachma. Enchantment is on a different curve: When you enchant people, your goal is not to make money from them or to get them to do what you want, but to fill them with great delight. Here are situations when you need enchantment the most:

- **Aspiring to lofty, idealistic results.** Want to change the world? Change caterpillars into butterflies? This takes more than run-of-the-mill relationships. You need to convince people to dream the same dream that you do.
- **Making difficult, infrequent decisions.** The greater the difficulty of the change, the greater the need for enchantment. Factors that cause friction include cost, risk, and politics. If a change is a big deal, then it's a big deal to make it happen.

- **Overcoming entrenched habits.** Most of the time, habits simplify life and enable fast, safe, and good decisions. But they can also prevent the adoption of a new idea that challenges the status quo. Enchantment can open the door for consideration of such a change.
- **Defying a crowd.** The crowd isn't always wise. It can lead you down a path of silliness, suboptimal choices, and downright destruction. Enchantment is as necessary to get people to diverge from a crowd as it is to get them to join one.
- **Proceeding despite delayed or nonexistent feedback.** A high level of dedication is necessary when feedback is rare or not readily available, and your efforts take a long time to see results. In these cases, moderate interest and support aren't enough. You must delight people so that they stick with you. For example, working for a biotech company takes a great deal of faith, because bringing new drugs to market can take ten years or more.

Do any of these situations sound familiar? They should, because they are present whenever people are trying to make the world a better place.

What Are People Thinking?

During the 1980s, Apple failed to sell Macintoshes to the business market. The fundamental flaw of our approach was that we did not understand what potential customers were thinking. Indeed, we believed they should leave the thinking to us.

We were so enchanted by our own product that we could not understand why everyone else did not feel the same way. That's when I learned that one must understand what people are thinking, feeling, and believing in order to enchant them.

The fix is to imagine yourself as the person you want to enchant and ask the following questions. If you can't come up with reasonable answers, don't expect your enchantment to work.

- **What does this person want?** You can't blame someone for wondering what your motives are. This doesn't mean that you should not benefit, but you should disclose your motivation to put her at ease.
- **Is the change worth the effort?** The next step is to help her understand how your cause ties in to what she wants. The benefits of change must outweigh the costs of change and the benefits of staying the same. The fact that you think change is worthwhile is not enough; the person you're trying to enchant must believe this, too.
- **Can I change?** Even if change is worthwhile, can she do it? Factors that prevent the change include the expense, effort, and risk that your change requires. She may doubt that she can change even if she wants to and believes it's worth it.

In the case of Apple in the 1980s, our motivation was to sell computers. We thought switching to Macintosh was worth the effort because of the gains in productivity and creativity. But we underestimated the difficulty of altering corporate policies and overcoming the perception that the Macintosh was easy to use but wimpy in terms of raw computational power.

By putting yourself in the mind-set of the people you're trying to enchant, you'll appreciate the amount of change that enchantment requires. It can take weeks or months for enchantment to occur, so prepare for a marathon, not a sprint.

Where Should You Draw the Line?

Enchantment is not about getting your way solely for your own benefit. To the contrary, if you want enchantment to last, other people must benefit, too. You also need to draw a bright line between ethical and unethical activities. Here's a gut check to determine which side of the line you're on:

- **Are you asking people to do something that you wouldn't do?** If you won't do something, don't ask others to do it, either. Asking people to do what you wouldn't do is called manipulation or coercion, not enchantment, and it doesn't work in the long run.

- **Do your interests conflict?** Enchantment endures if your interests are aligned with the interests of your constituencies. Alignment makes enchantment both ethical and more enjoyable. If your interests aren't aligned, you should either alter your interests or rethink your intended market.

- **Have you hidden your conflicts of interest?** Even if your interests are aligned—according to you, anyway—you should disclose your stake as an employee, shareholder, or other form of interested party. There's no such thing as too much disclosure.

- **Are you telling "noble lies"?** The slope is slippery when the big picture or the greater good seems to justify the means. There is no such thing, however, as a "noble lie." There are lies and truths—and nothing in between.

- **Are you enchanting gullible people?** Enchanting gullible people—folks who don't have the ability to discern the truth or what's best for them—is immoral. Fooling gullible people is easy and happens every day, but do not mistake this for success. Also, enchanting gullible people doesn't improve your skills. It will, however, give you a false sense of competence and maybe turn you into a crook.

If you answer yes to any of these questions, then you're an unethical enchanter. Your efforts might work for a short while, but the karmic scoreboard in the sky will catch up to you. Take this opportunity to transform your enchantment and to leave the dark side.

Examples and How to Use This Book

> Behavioral psychology is the science of pulling
> habits out of rats. —Douglas Busch

In the course of writing *Enchantment*, I read dozens of books about persuading, influencing, and wooing people. Many of these books cite psychology studies to "prove" why you should use various techniques. When I could, I read the original papers and reports, and I learned a few things:

- In much of the research, undergraduate students were the experimental subjects. If not students, the subjects were rats or mice. They (college students) represented a small segment of the population, and making a few bucks or receiving course credits was often the motivation. Results from these studies can apply to real-world cases, but you shouldn't assume they do.
- Scientists were looking for a "statistically significant" difference between a control group and an experimental group, a difference that they could not attribute to chance. Their salient question was, "If we were to run this study again, what are the odds we'd get the same result?" Statistical significance, however, does not always reveal how large the difference is between the control and experimental groups. Scientists call this difference the effect size.
- The people who conducted the research were scientists, and scientists try to understand and explain the world. They care about good scientific research: controls of variables, objectivity, repeatability, fame, and funding.

You probably aren't a scientist. You probably don't care about statistically significant good science that holds up under peer review. You probably do care about a big effect size. And even if you prefer scientific controls, let's face reality: time constraints, competitive reactions, seasonality, consumer moods, and clueless managers are already keeping you busy.

The truth is, there is limited black-and-white, scientific proof of many enchantment techniques, and that's OK, because the right attitude is: "This technique is interesting. Maybe it applies to us. Let's see if it works." The way to use *Enchantment* is to try these ideas, modify and adapt them as you go, abandon the losers, and run with

the winners. I am going to show you how to change the world, not understand it.

Personal Stories

One of my favorite parts of magazine articles is the little story within the story, called a sidebar or callout. Done well, these stories are like a scoop of vanilla ice cream on top of a slice of apple pie.

During the final stages of writing this book, I asked people to send me personal examples of enchantment. Each chapter ends with one of these stories to illustrate real-world enchantment in the person's own words. The stories often relate to the subject of the chapter but not always. Sometimes I just thought they were cool.

My Personal Story, by Eric Dawson

Eric Dawson is a higher-education senior strategic accounts manager for Apple in Oklahoma City, Oklahoma. In this personal story, he explains how a Macintosh enchanted him in the midst of a tragedy.

MY STORY IS HOW I CAME TO WORK FOR APPLE. IN 1996 MY SON, Seth, was born with a terminal neurological disorder called lissencephaly. He couldn't walk, talk, or sit up, and we had to tube-feed him. We were unable to teach him "cause and effect."

I set Seth in front of a Macintosh Performa running a custom program connected to a game paddle. One minute of *The Lion King* would play, and then the computer would freeze. Restarting required tapping the paddle.

One day I came into the room without him knowing, and I saw him teach himself to hit the paddle. It was the proudest moment of my life. I went to work for Apple one month later. Seth passed away fifteen days after I started, but he had done his job. To this day I help empower people as an Apple employee.

Chapter 2
How to Achieve Likability

Some cause happiness wherever they go; others,
whenever they go.

—Oscar Wilde

N ow that you understand the importance of enchantment, we can build a foundation to implement it. Step one is achieving likability, because jerks seldom enchant people. It's true that a magnificent cause can overcome a prickly personality, but why make things harder? This chapter explains how to make yourself more likable.

Make Crow's-Feet

Let's start with the first impression that you make. Four factors create a good one: your smile, your dress, your handshake, and your vocabulary. First, smile at people. What does it cost to smile? Nothing. What does it cost not to smile? Everything, if it prevents you from connecting with people. While smiling sends a very clear message about your state of mind, not smiling creates an opening for many interpretations, including grumpiness, aloofness, and anger—none of which helps you enchant people. If you don't believe smiling is useful, answer these questions:

- Do you like to do business with grumpy people?
- Do you know anyone who does?
- Do you think grumpy people get what they want?

The key to a great, George Clooneyesque smile is to think pleasant thoughts. If you're grumpy inside, it's hard to have a smile that lights up a room. The most you'll accomplish is a fake smile, and a fake smile won't make people like you.

© Vera Anderson / Wire Image / Getty Images

A fake smile uses only the zygomatic major muscle—the one that runs from your jaw to the corner of your mouth. It's easy to control this muscle, so it leads to fake or what was called "Pan American smiles" (called this because Pan American flight attendants supposedly weren't truly happy to see passengers).

A great smile uses the orbicularis oculi muscle, too. This muscle surrounds your eyes, and it makes you squint and produces crow's-feet. A real smile is so special that it has its own name: the Duchenne smile, in honor of Guillaume Duchenne, a French neurologist.

So when you meet people, think pleasant thoughts, fire up the orbicularis oculi muscle, and make crow's-feet so deep they can hold water. Call them laugh lines instead, if this makes you feel better. And for the sake of your smile, skip the Botox treatments and face-lifts.

Dress for a Tie

Distrust any enterprise that requires new clothes.

—Henry David Thoreau

The second factor is how you dress. This is the one time you want a tie (no pun intended), not a victory or a loss. Overdressing says, "I'm richer, more powerful, and more important than you." Under-dressing says, "I don't respect you. I'll dress any way that I please." Equal dressing says, "We're peers." My recommendation is to park your ego. You don't have to "make a statement" and try to show people you have money, power, or great taste. The goal is likability—not superiority.

That said, your dress shouldn't conflict with what you stand for. For example, if you're an outside-the-box, innovative, and revolu-tionary thinker, then a three-piece suit with a bow tie won't cut it. In the same way, if you're the adult supervision, then a T-shirt and jeans won't work, either.

Dressing for a tie while staying true to your message can create an issue: What if matching your audience conflicts with your message? For example, should you wear jeans or a suit when you're the adult supervision in a company with a jeans–and–T-shirt atmosphere?

John Sculley faced this issue when he came to work at Apple. He chose to embrace the jeans look although he was the adult supervision.

I don't think he was ever comfortable in jeans, and employees never considered him "one of the guys."

If you encounter this situation, here are two recommendations: First, ask people in the organization what to do. At least this shows you are smart enough to ask and flexible enough to listen—which are both valuable messages in themselves.

Second, except for cases where doing so is organizational suicide, dress in a manner that makes you feel comfortable. It's hard to enchant people when you're uncomfortable, and besides, there's something enchanting about a person who is who she is and lets it rip.

Perfect Your Handshake

The third factor in first impressions is your handshake. Fortunately, Geoffrey Beattie, head of psychological sciences at the University of Manchester, came up with this formula for the perfect handshake:

$PH = \sqrt{(e2 + ve2)(d2) + (cg + dr)2 + \pi\{(4 < s > 2)(4 < p > 2)\}2 + (vi + t + te)2 + \{(4 < c > 2)(4 < du > 2)\}2}$

Where *e* is eye contact (1=none, 5=direct), optimum value 5; *ve* is verbal greeting (1=totally inappropriate, 5=totally appropriate), 5; *d* is Duchenne smile—smiling in eyes and mouth, plus symmetry on both sides of face, and slower offset (1=totally non-Duchenne smile or false smile, 5=totally Duchenne), 5; *cg* completeness of grip (1=very incomplete, 5=full), 5; *dr* is dryness of hand (1=damp, 5=dry), 4; *s* is strength (1=weak, 5=strong), 3; *p* is position of hand (1=back toward own body, 5=in other person's bodily zone), 3; *vi* is vigor (1=too low/too high, 5=mid), 3; *t* is temperature of hands (1=too cold/too hot; 5=mid), 3; *te* is texture of hands (1=too rough/too smooth, 5=mid), 3; *c* is control (1=low; 5=high), 3; and *du* is duration (1= brief; 5=long), 3.*

---

* "Scientists Devise Guide to the Perfect Handshake," Physorg.com (blog), July 16, 2010, www.physorg.com/news198475137.html.

If you weren't a math major, allow me to translate this equation into plain English:

- Make eye contact throughout.
- Utter an appropriate verbal greeting.
- Make a Duchenne smile.
- Grip the person's hand and give it a firm squeeze.
- Stand a moderate distance from the other person: not so close as to make him uncomfortable or so far away as to make him feel detached.
- Make sure your hand is cool, dry, and smooth.
- Use a medium level of vigor.
- Hold the handshake for no longer than two to three seconds.

We're almost done with creating a great first impression. The next step is to work on the words that you use when speaking to people.

Use the Right Words

The fourth factor is your vocabulary. Words are the facial expressions of your mind: They communicate your attitude, personality, and perspective. Wrong words give the wrong impression, so heed these recommendations:

- **Use simple words.** When you use words people have to look up in a dictionary or search for in Wikipedia, you've failed. As the Danish proverb goes, "Big words seldom accompany good deeds."
- **Use the active voice.** Consider the impact of these two phrases: "Use the right words" versus "The right words should be used by you." The passive voice is wimpy and inefficient. Enchanters use the active voice.
- **Keep it short.** In ten years of listening to entrepreneurs' pitches, I've never heard one that was too short. If people are interested, they'll ask for more information. If they're not, providing more

information won't sway them, so use fewer words to express yourself.

- **Use common, unambiguous analogies.** Two common analogies that people use are war and sports. On war: Many people have not fought in a war, and those who have will tell you that war is confusion, death, and pain more than glory, victory, and leadership. Also, wars have a winner and a loser, whereas the goal of enchantment is mutually assured satisfaction. Finally, war analogies are ineffective at enchanting women.

  On sports: Sports analogies, on the other hand, are effective because many people of both genders play sports. Nevertheless, sports are specific to countries—try using a cricket analogy on Americans,* "It's third down and ten, so we need to go deep" on Indians, or "We'll deke the competition and go topshelf" on South Americans. If in doubt, use analogies that are specific to the culture of your audience or stick to common ones involving kids and family life.

People often overlook the choice of words, like the choice of clothing, when they present themselves. The list of fundamentals is now complete: smile, dress, handshake, and words. We can move on to our attitude.

Accept Others

For people to like you, they have to accept you. For people to accept you, you have to accept them. Here are four observations that will help you accept others in case you have difficulty doing so:

- **People are not binary.** People are not ones or zeros, smart or dumb, worthwhile or worthless. Everyone has strengths and weaknesses, positives and negatives, competencies and deficiencies.

---

* I don't know enough about cricket to provide an example!

- **Everyone is better than you at something.** People who don't accept others often think they are superior to everyone. But no one is superior to everyone in every way. You may be a rich investment banker, but the person you look down upon may be a great teacher.
- **People are more similar than they are different.** At a basic level, almost everyone wants to raise a family, do something meaningful, and enjoy life. This is true across races, cultures, creeds, colors, and countries. If you looked, you would discover that you have a lot in common with people whom you don't like.
- **People deserve a break.** The stressed and unorganized person who doesn't have the same priorities as you may be dealing with an autistic child, abusive spouse, fading parents, or cancer. Don't judge people until you've walked a kilometer in their shoes. Give them a break instead.

Death is the great equalizer—we all die equal as a lump of tissue, bone, and fluid. While we're living, we need to get over ourselves and accept others if we want to enchant people.

Get Close

Are the people you like the ones you see all the time? Maybe there's something else going on. Maybe the fact that you see them often is the reason you've come to like them.

Close proximity and frequent contact mean you interact with them more, and your relationship can more easily progress from acquaintance to friend because of casual and spontaneous encounters. In other words, presence makes the heart grow fonder.

Unfortunately, large companies, virtual organizations, and digital communication work against physical proximity. Electronic/virtual/digital interaction is good for maintaining relationships, but pressing flesh is better for creating relationships. This is the main reason to get out of your chair and jump into the analog world.

Companies like Zappos, the online shoe company, have figured

The enchanted and enchanting Zappos crew.

out ways to fight isolation. For example, Zappos employees work in an open, few-walls environment that they personalize to the hilt. Zappos also turned the employee entrances and exits at its Las Vegas building into emergency-only exits, so people bump into each other at the main entrance.

Zappos even digitized closeness for its far-flung workforce. After Zappos employees enter their name and password in the computer system, the software presents them with a picture of a randomly selected colleague. Employees then take a multiple-choice test to name the person. After they make a selection, the system displays the person's profile and bio.

The Brafman brothers, in their book *Click: The Magic of Instant Connections,* sum up the principle this way: ". . . the single most important factor in determining whether or not you connect with another person is neither personality nor mutual interests—it is simple proximity."* So get up and EBWA (enchant by wandering around).

---

* Ori Brafman and Rom Brafman, *Click: The Magic of Instant Connections* (New York: Broadway Business, 2010), 61.

Don't Impose Your Values

> I wish they would only take me as I am.
>
> —Vincent van Gogh

A health organization once tried to scare teens from smoking marijuana by telling them that young people who smoked it were five times more likely to engage in sex. Think about that: Would this pitch encourage or discourage teenagers from smoking the evil weed?

At best, the answer is, "Not clear." This example illustrates the danger of projecting your values on others: Doing so can lead to the opposite of what you're trying to accomplish. At the least, it might make people resent your heavy-handedness.

Instances of people imposing values on others and still succeeding in enchanting them are rare. Maybe they bludgeoned folks into submission, but that's not enchantment, and they can only sustain submission through brute force. Truly, the best enchanters savor the differences among people's values and use an inclusive model.

The positioning of Facebook is an example of not imposing values. Early on, the service focused on the youth market and a student-centric customer base. Over time, Facebook abandoned this focus and concentrated on an inclusive model for people of all ages. As a result, multiple generations of families are now on the service, and Facebook has more users than the populations of most countries.

Pursue and Project Your Passions

In the village of Auvers-sur-Oise, nineteen miles (thirty kilometers) outside Paris, there is a small house called Auberge Ravoux. This is where Vincent van Gogh lived before he committed suicide in 1890. He finished seventy-five paintings in the last few months of his life in the village.

On July 21, 1985, Dominique-Charles Janssens was in a car accident in front of Auberge Ravoux. When he reviewed the accident report, he learned of the significance of the location and became intrigued. One thing led to another, and in 1987 he purchased the property. Over time, his family invested $6.4 million (€5 million) in its restoration, and he is the president of Institut Van Gogh, the organization that operates the facility.

Janssens is a historian, restaurateur, and Van Gogh evangelist. He has dedicated his life to the preservation of Van Gogh's memory and to make Van Gogh's wish come true: "Some day or other I believe I shall find a way of having an exhibition of my own in a café." Janssens lives and breathes Van Gogh, and that makes him a world-class enchanter. He is the most passionate person I've ever met, and I've met thousands of passionate people.

Janssens enchanting his guests.

Janssens is a great example of how pursuing and projecting your passions can make you enchanting. Some people, like Janssens, dedicate themselves to their passions. Others supplement their lives with additional passions:

Name	Position	Passions
Scott McNealy	Co-founder of Sun Microsystems	Hockey and golf. He built a rink in his backyard in Silicon Valley.
Bill Ford	Executive chairman of the board, Ford Motor Company	Tae kwon do, hockey, and folk guitar ("Billy Got Back" is his biggest hit).
Norio Ohga	CEO of Sony	Opera. He got a job at Sony because he complained about the quality of Sony's tape recorders.
George S. Patton	General of U.S. Army	Sailing. Patton's boat was called the *When and If,* referring to when and if Patton returned from World War II.
Tim Ferris	Author of *The 4-Hour Work Week*	Breakdancing, of all things.
Albert Einstein	Physicist	Violin: "I know that the most joy in my life has come to me from my violin."
Geena Davis	Actress	Archery. She came in 24th out of 300 women trying out for the 2000 Olympics USA archery team.
Guy Kawasaki	Good question	Hockey.

What are your passions? Do you hide them under a bushel? Instead, tell the world that you love cooking, hockey, NASCAR, or knitting—whatever it is—because pursuing your passions makes you more interesting, and interesting people are enchanting.

Find Shared Passions

Two social scientists from England named Neil Rackham and John Carlisle found that the best negotiators spend 40 percent of their preparation time finding shared interests with the other party.* Do you invest this much effort when you interact with people?

The first step to finding shared passions is to pursue and project your own passions, as I explained above. Then you can accelerate finding shared passions by taking these steps:

- **Assume everyone has passions.** Everyone is passionate about something. It's your job to find out what it is. Good starting points are kids, sports, travel, and food. If the person has no passions, he might not be worth enchanting.

- **Assume you have something in common.** If you assume you share interests with people, you will find them. If you assume you don't, you won't find anything, because you will give up too easily.

- **Do your homework.** A successful enchanter is a diligent one. Back in the day, people had to make trips to the library to read back issues of newspapers and magazines and out-of-date directories to learn about people. Now you can search for people on Google, read their walls on Facebook, access their profiles on LinkedIn, and read their latest thoughts on Twitter to find shared interests.

Finding shared passions is a great tool to developing relationships. In my case, when strangers tell me they play hockey, they lower my resistance to their pitch because we have something in common. If nothing else, I respect them for making the effort to learn my passion.

In many cases I've ended up playing hockey with them and then listening to their pitch. I learned about their business, and they

---

* Richard G. Shell and Mario Moussa, *The Art of Woo: Using Strategic Persuasion to Sell Your Ideas* (New York: Portfolio, 2007), 156.

learned that I'm a much better evangelist than a hockey player. The point is that finding shared passions breaks down barriers.

Create Win-Win Situations

Likable people create win-win outcomes in which everyone gains something. Neile McQueen Toffel, Steve McQueen's first wife, told this great story to my friend Jon Winokur, author of *The Portable Curmudgeon*. Late in 1963, Paul Newman, James Garner, Steve McQueen, and Neile went to a car race in Riverside, California.

On the way back to Los Angeles, Neile had to use the bathroom, so she insisted that they stop at a service station. Unfortunately, the line for the ladies' room was long, and Neile knew the men would get angry because they wanted to beat the traffic back to the city.

So she went up to the girls standing in line and said, "Hey, do you know there's a car full of movie stars around the bend?"

"Who?" they asked in unison.

"Why, there's Steve McQueen, there's Paul Newman, and there's James Garner!" said Neile.

With that, the girls looked at one another and ran like crazy to the car. Neile didn't have to wait in a line anymore, and she never told the actors how the girls found them.

This was a win-win-win: Neile got into the bathroom, the girls met some famous movie stars, and the men got back on the road in less time. One way to get people to like you is to create win-win outcomes.

Swear

> Taboo words persist because they can intensify emotional communication to a degree that nontaboo words cannot.
>
> —Timothy Jay

Swearing can arouse attention, build solidarity, demonstrate strength, release tension, and convey informality, so it can increase your acceptance by all but very prudish people. For example, on June 6, 2009, Leo Laporte, founder of a tech news site called This Week in Technology, and Michael Arrington, founder of another tech news site called TechCrunch, got into an argument on a podcast called *The Gillmor Gang*. Leo mentioned how much he liked a new phone called the Pre, from Palm, and this conversation took place:

Arrington: Hold on, hold on. Did you pay for the Pre? Let's get the disclosures out of the way right away.

Laporte: This is a one-week review unit. I couldn't get one and unfortunately I don't think I'll be able to get one. I was going to get one this afternoon.

Arrington: OK, so you got a free Pre. You're one of the few people that got a Pre.

Laporte: Not at all. I think quite a few reviewers got one. Yeah, Scoble has one. Mike, that's really BS, and I'm really pissed off that you would imply that in some way that this quote, free Pre, that I send back in seven days, would in any way predispose me. Screw you.

Arrington: What are you going to do about it?

Laporte: Mike, you are such a troll. Screw you. I'm not kidding, screw you, you asshole, screw you.

Arrington: I don't think he's being serious.

Laporte: I'm being very serious, Mike, that's bullshit.

Arrington: How is it bullshit?

Laporte: I'm infuriated. I'm infuriated that you would imply that because I have a review unit, that would somehow influence me. Screw you. I'm throwing you all off. F&#! you, guys.

As I read the situation, Arrington knew perfectly well that companies send new products to people like Laporte. In fact, Arrington probably gets as much stuff from companies as Laporte. Arrington was trying to create a controversy for the sake of creating a controversy even though he knew that Laporte had done nothing improper.

Laporte's use of profanity showed that he was just a regular guy who wasn't going to put up with bull shiitake. Over the next few days, hundreds of people wrote in to support what he had done. If you're going to swear, however, you must abide by these rules so that it doesn't work against you:

- **Swear infrequently.** People who swear on a daily basis come off as crude, and when used regularly, profanity loses its effectiveness. Laporte seldom swears during his appearances, so the audience knew he was upset by Arrington's assertion.
- **Swear only in cases of forehead-smacking hypocrisy, arrogance, intentional inaccuracy, and dishonesty.** In other words, you typically don't swear but you couldn't control yourself in a particular instance. Arrington's insinuations, for example, were hypocritical and inaccurate and merited a harshly worded response instead of a polite one. (This is called dysphemistic swearing, if you want to impress someone with your knowledge of the intricacies of profanity.)*
- **Swear only when the audience supports you.** Swearing seldom works if the audience isn't positively inclined to you and your message. It usually backfires and makes a hostile audience even more hostile. The Gillmor Gang show was running on Laporte's site, and he was the host that day. Most of the people who watch the show are there because they like him. As the quantity of supportive e-mails showed, the audience clearly supported Laporte.

---

* Dr. Steven Pinker, "The Stuff of Thought: Language as a Window into Human Nature," September 10, 2008, www.youtube.com/watch?v=yyNmGHpL11Q.

- **Soften your profanity.** Use words like *crap* and *suck*, which are strong enough to do the trick but are less likely to offend anyone. You can also do what I do and use *bull shiitake* as my go-to swear word—it's technically a special kind of bovine mushroom, not profanity. And if someone is a real jerk, you can always call him an orifice without using the a-hole word.

Swearing is not without risk, but you cannot build rapport with people without taking risks, so drop a few swear-bombs when the situation genuinely calls for it, and see what happens. Do not, however, swear to intimidate or humiliate a person if you want to make swearing work for you. This is simply unacceptable.

A word to women regarding swearing. Circa 2010, there is still a double standard, and it is less socially acceptable for women to swear than men. Hence, many women feel comfortable swearing only in the presence of other women or with people who are their peers. My advice is that you heed the rules that I provided above, and let it rip, because the best way to destroy a double standard is to defy it.

Default to Yes

The final way to become likable is to adopt a yes attitude. This means your default response to people's requests is yes. Don't be alarmed: This isn't a risky practice, because most requests at the beginning of a relationship are small, simple, and easy.

A yes buys time, enables you to see more options, and builds rapport. I learned this from ace schmoozer Darcy Rezac, author of *The Frog and the Prince: Secrets of Positive Networking*. He defines good networking as always thinking about how you can help people when you meet them.

By contrast, a no response stops everything. There's no place to go, nothing to build on, and no further options are available. You will never know what may have come out of a relationship if you don't let it begin. At least, think "not yet" instead of no.

To make a default yes work, you must assume people are reasonable, honest, and grateful. Everyone isn't always reasonable, honest, and grateful, but most people are, and you can live your life in one of two ways: thinking people are bad until proven good or thinking they're good until proven bad.

Take my word for it: More people will like you if you believe people are good until proven bad.

My Personal Story, by Fran Shea

Fran Shea is the former president of E! Entertainment Television in Los Angeles, California. In this personal story, she explains how Howard Stern's likability enchanted her.

IT BEGAN AS DESPERATION: I WAS TWELVE MONTHS INTO BUILDING the programming plan for E! Entertainment Television back in the early nineties. I was head of programming. We needed a big move.

The idea: *The Howard Stern Show*. The obstacles:

- His radio popularity was climbing because he had just launched in Los Angeles on a popular radio station. His stations, once East Coast based, were multiplying, because his show was simulcast in more and more cities, so he didn't need an affiliation with an unknown start-up on his résumé.
- He was discouraged by a recent attempt at television, having been disappointed by the producers and executives at a local venue. He was very put off by television.
- He was tremendously busy. His show was four to five hours per day, five days a week plus production and meetings. He was also a dedicated family man.
- He was in New York. E! was in Los Angeles.
- He was *waaaaay* too expensive for our little cable channel.
- His agent is among the smartest in our business.

A meeting was set. There was magic in the air. Howard was charming. I was enchanted by a man whose reputation doesn't conjure that expectation. The meeting was funny and light, and I was surprised because I had bought into his shock-jock reputation. Howard was disarming, with all the talent of a seasoned comedian (which he is). Howard's persona masks his professionalism.

Enchantment comes in many disguises, it seems. It turns out that my desperation fueled a great pitch. I was certain I could erase his objections about putting his radio show on the air. I had worked with many comedians over the years as a producer at HBO, and I could tell he was a very talented performer.

I went into sell mode. There was an incredibly unlikely meeting of the minds. I remember a lot of laughter as we began to position ourselves for an eventual deal. This was the surprise: This meeting was *so* important to me, but I was having so much fun. I guess it was because a deal was so unlikely that the meeting was so unusual, so light, so "enchanting"!

We genuinely liked each other, and I believe it became obvious we could do something "different" together. Howard is all about "different." Over time, we crafted a deal that would help put E! on the map, and *The Howard Stern Show* ran nightly for many years on E!

Chapter 3

How to Achieve Trustworthiness

> Every sale has five basic obstacles: no need, no money,
> no hurry, no desire, no trust.
>
> **—Zig Ziglar**

Likability is half the battle of the enchanting new you. The other half is achieving trustworthiness, because people can like someone but not trust him enough for enchantment to occur. This chapter explains how you can deserve and gain the genuine trust of others.

Trust Others

If Tony Hsieh, the CEO of Zappos and author of *Delivering Happiness: A Path to Passion, Profits, and Purpose,* had told me that he was starting a business that depended on women buying shoes without trying them on, I would have told him he was nuts. I mean, there was no way my wife would buy shoes this way. I was wrong, and there's a constant flow of Zappos boxes into our house as well as the houses of thousands of other women (and men).

Zappos is built on trust—two-way trust, actually. Women trust Zappos's money-back guarantee with free shipping in both directions, and Zappos trusts women not to abuse this privilege by returning shoes they have used.

People who don't trust others have often had bad experiences that cause them to embrace a distrusting, kill-or-be-killed philosophy. However, if you want people to trust you, you have to trust them.

Consider what you have to look forward to: When people trust each other, they stop playing games, they look beyond temporary problems, and they expose themselves with less hesitation. Good enchanters are likable, but great enchanters are likable *and* trustworthy.

Get this right: The first step is to trust others—as Zappos trusted its customers not to abuse the ability to return shoes with free shipping. The rest of this chapter explains how to increase your own trustworthiness and hence your ability to enchant.

Be a Mensch

> We should give as we would receive, cheerfully, quickly, and without hesitation; for there is no grace in a benefit that sticks to the fingers.   —**Seneca**

Mensch is a German word for "human being," but its Yiddish connotation far exceeds this definition. If you are a mensch, you are honest, fair, kind, and transparent, no matter whom you're dealing with and who will ever know what you did. My buddy Bruna Martinuzzi, author of *The Leader as a Mensch: Become the Kind of Person Others Want to Follow,* compiled a list of ten ways to achieve menschdom.* Here is my paraphrase of her insights:

---

* Bruna Martinuzzi, "How to Be a Mensch in Business," Open Forum (blog), April 3, 2009, www.openforum.com/idea-hub/topics/the-world/article/how-to-be-a-mensch-in-business-guy-kawasaki.

1. Always act with honesty.
2. Treat people who have wronged you with civility.
3. Fulfill your unkept promises from the past.
4. Help someone who can be of absolutely no use to you.
5. Suspend blame when something goes wrong and ask, "What can we learn?"
6. Hire people who are as smart as or smarter than you and give them opportunities for growth.
7. Don't interrupt people; don't dismiss their concerns offhand; don't rush to give advice; don't change the subject. Allow people their moment.
8. Do no harm in anything you undertake.
9. Don't be too quick to shoot down others' ideas.
10. Share your knowledge, expertise, and best practices with others.

I'd add two more ways to achieve menschdom:

- **Focus on goodwill.** Mensches focus on goodwill—that is, positive actions that make the world a better place. People distrust those who focus on improving their own position and who denigrate others.
- **Give people the benefit of the doubt.** You know that my theory is that people are good until proven bad. I also believe that several bad experiences are necessary to prove anyone bad. My backup theory is that good people can do bad things because of circumstances that I don't understand. This doesn't mean they are bad people.

Jon Winokur, the author who told me Neile McQueen Toffel's story about the service-station bathroom line, got to know her because he's the coauthor of James Garner's biography, *The Garner Files: A Memoir.* (The McQueens were friends of Garner.)

Coauthors usually get a flat fee with no royalty for this kind of project. One day Garner's manager called Winokur and said, "Jim told me to tell you that he wants the book to be a fifty-fifty split all the way down the line," and a few weeks later Winokur received the contract with Garner's signature already on it.

Winokur is also a mensch because he acknowledged and thanked Garner for the generosity. When Winokur did this, Garner asked, "What generosity?"

Winokur replied, "You've just handed me half of a very valuable property when you could have had me for a fraction of it."

"Really?" Garner asked, "Why didn't you tell me before?" Of course Garner knew what he was doing all along, but he was too gracious to take credit for it. In other words, Garner was saying, "Don't menschion it."

If you want people to remember you as a person who helped others and made the world a better place, be a mensch. It's that simple.

Disclose Your Interests

Immediate and complete disclosure of your interests is a key component of trustworthiness. As I mentioned earlier, people will always wonder what your motivation is, so you should get this out of the way.

Most people won't care that you are an interested or conflicted party as long as you disclose the relationship. We all need to make a living. Damage to your trustworthiness occurs if people believe that you don't have any financial interests and find out later that you do.

Also, if you're trying to enchant people because you love a cause, disclosure is good marketing. It means you believe in the cause so much that you have chosen to work for it. For example, I list the companies that I have invested in or advise on my blog. I even call the list my Alignment of Interests, as opposed to Conflicts of Interests, because I believe my interests are aligned with the interests of both my readers and these companies.

Give for Intrinsic Reasons

According to Robert B. Cialdini, author of *Influence: The Psychology of Persuasion*, retired professor from Arizona State University, and all-around godfather of influence, the government of Ethiopia sent money to Mexico after an earthquake struck the country in 1985. Ethiopia did this despite its own crushing economic hardships, because Mexico had supported Ethiopia after an Italian invasion fifty years earlier.

Ethiopia's action is an example of reciprocity, the act of returning a favor, a gift, or assistance. There are three forms of reciprocity. The first occurs when you do something with the explicit, quid pro quo expectation of receiving something in return. This is a transaction, and it can work, but it isn't enchantment.

The second form of reciprocity involves doing something as an investment in the future or "paying it forward." This isn't a transaction, because the give and the get are not explicit and closely timed. In fact, the reciprocation may never occur, but there's the possibility that it could. This type of reciprocation can create enchantment.

The third form of reciprocation occurs when you do something for intrinsic reasons, such as helping others. This is the purest form of reciprocity, because recipients often cannot repay you—for example, someone lying on the side of the road to Jericho. But as my mother used to say, *"Akua sabe"* (the gods know). This form of reciprocity increases your trustworthiness the most and causes the most enchantment.

Gain Knowledge and Competence

Knowledge means you have expertise, thanks to your education or experience. Evidence of knowledge includes academic degrees, employment history, customer references, certifications, awards, and other forms of recognition.

Competence is different from knowledge, because knowing is not the same as doing. Competence means that you have progressed beyond knowing what to do, to doing what you know. I struggled to find an example of knowledge and competence until I realized that I was listening to one almost every day: Terry Gross, executive producer and host of *Fresh Air* on National Public Radio.

Gross personifies enchantment with her low-key, conversational yet probing interviews. The *San Francisco Chronicle* described her interviews as "a remarkable blend of empathy, warmth, genuine curiosity, and sharp intelligence." She is knowledge *and* competence.

If you listen to National Public Radio on the weekends, there's also Peter Sagal demonstrating the same knowledge and competence on *Wait Wait . . . Don't Tell Me!*, the news quiz show. Sagal is an accomplished playwright, but who cares about that? He is amazing at coming up with the instant, priceless retort. No one skewers rich, famous, and powerful people for their stupidity, arrogance, and cluelessness better than he:

> When Tony Hayward took the reins of BP in 2007, he pledged to fix the company's safety problems, and priority number one was avoiding unpleasant coffee burns. Priority number four hundred: not ruining the world.
>
> So at BP, many hallways at their headquarters have a sign imploring employees not to walk and carry coffee at the same time. Workplace hot-beverage-related incidents are way down. So following the success of that coffee safety plan, crews are now posting signs on all their deepwater wells, saying, "Please do not spill all the oil into the ocean." (July 17, 2010)

Knowledge is great. Competence is great. But the combination of both encourages people to trust you and increases your powers of enchantment. And in this world, the combination is a breath of fresh air.

Show Up

You can embody the qualities of menschdom, knowledge, and competence, but they won't matter if you don't show up—that is, interact with people. In digital-speak, showing up means answering your e-mails, tweets, voicemails, and video chats, but let me begin with a well-known story about starfish.

In the Loren Eiseley tale "The Star Thrower," a traveler sees a man throwing starfish back into the sea to save them. He asks him why he thinks he can make a difference, since there are thousands of starfish on the beach. He picks up another, throws it into the ocean, and says, "It makes a difference to that one."

Every day I get a total of two hundred e-mails, tweets, letters, and voicemails. I don't answer them all, but I come closer than most people. For those to whom I respond, "it makes a difference." Even if my response is no more than, "Sorry, I can't help you right now," recipients often write me back to thank me.

If you want people to trust you, show up physically and virtually. It's a humongous amount of work, but you can't establish trust with thousands of people in short spans of time. It takes many months to establish a halo of trustworthiness.

Bake a Bigger Pie

There are two kinds of people and organizations in the world: eaters and bakers. Eaters want a bigger slice of an existing pie; bakers want to make a bigger pie. Eaters think that if they win, you lose, and if you win, they lose. Bakers think that everyone can win with a bigger pie.

Twitter made a bigger pie because anyone could provide news and updates. Southwest Airlines moved people from cars and buses to airplanes. Google wrested advertising out of the hands of agencies and gave it to small businesses. All these companies baked a bigger pie instead of eating more of the same pie.

Baking a bigger pie increases your trustworthiness and yields these benefits:

- **People work together.** Even your competitors will work with you, because everyone can benefit, and the more people working on an idea, the better the results for everyone.
- **The "state of the art" progresses and changes.** If the pie stays the same, then progress comes to a halt. If the pie gets bigger, then new technology and ideas reach fruition.
- **Customers increase in number and diversity.** When a pie gets bigger, there are more users of products and services. With the democratization of computers and the Internet, more people used them, and many more people benefited.

As the saying goes, "A rising tide floats all boats," and bakers are much more enchanting than eaters.

Enchant People on Their Own Terms

The Susan G. Komen Race for the Cure supports organizations trying to find a cure for breast cancer. There are several categories for race participants. Breast cancer survivors pay a $35 entry fee, and anyone else can run for $40. People can also walk for $35, and kids can run for $20—so far, so logical.

But did you know you can also "Sleep in for the Cure" for $35? (Advice to Susan G. Komen staffers: You should charge the most for this level of participation. This would relieve the guilt of people who did not want to get out of bed plus increase the amount of donations you collect.)

The lesson is to step back and enchant people on their own terms. Hardcore people want to get up at the crack of dawn and punish themselves by running. Others want to support you by sleeping in. Don't be picky, and take whatever help they give you. And optimize your pricing for everyone's benefit.

Position Yourself

A great man is one sentence.   —Clare Boothe Luce

The final step of likability and trustworthiness is to craft a description of you or your organization. It should explain what you do and why you exist. For guidance, here are the four qualities of a good positioning statement:

- **Short.** The fewer words, the better. Ten words is the limit. This applies to describing yourself as well as your organization. Think of your positioning statement as a mantra, not a wordy mission.
- **Clear.** Use simple terms anyone can understand, and answer the question, "What do you do?" Also, focus on your function, not your pompous title. The two are not the same.
- **Different.** Many people use words such as *dedicated, hardworking,* and *honest* to describe themselves. Find words that most people don't use, because no one describes himself as lazy or dishonest. Better still, cut out adjectives and use verbs to simply explain what you do.
- **Humble.** A personal positioning statement that isn't humble will reduce your credibility, so cool it on the narcissism. Another benefit of cutting out adjectives is that doing so will foster humility.

Even the simplest positioning can do wonders. For example, Steve Martin, coauthor of *Yes! 50 Scientifically Proven Ways to Be Persuasive,* told me about a real estate office that altered its telephone receptionists' script and increased face-to-face meetings by 20.1 percent and sales by 16 percent with only a slight adjustment.

The simple change consisted of adding phrases such as, "She has twenty years of experience in renting property in this area," to the usual "Let me connect you to Sandra." Mentioning the years of experience positioned the brokers so well that it increased their ability to acquire clients.

My positioning statement is two words: "Empower people." What's yours? Write it in this small space:

Be a Hero

> A hero is a man who is afraid to run away.
>
> **—English proverb**

I end this chapter with a way to push the limits of likability, trust-worthiness, and enchantment. The idea is to be a hero. People throw that term around like nickels—applying it to entrepreneurs, ath-letes, philanthropists, and politicians because they made lots of money, scored a last-minute touchdown, gave millions of dollars to charity, or ran for office. People should throw *hero* around like man-hole covers—applying it to men and women who do great things at great risk and demonstrate courage and fortitude under extreme conditions.

For example, an architect named Frank De Martini and three col-leagues named Pablo Ortiz, Carlos DaCosta, and Pete Negron saved seventy people before perishing in the 9/11 attack on the World Trade Center. A Japanese consulate official named Chiune Sugihara approved more than two thousand visas for Jews trying to escape the Nazis in Lithuania in 1940. His action was in direct defiance of the Japanese government and created grave personal danger for him and his wife. These folks were genuine heroes.

You, too, could be a hero. You don't need any special training or genetics. The first response of many heroes is to deny their special-ness and claim that "anyone would have done what I did in the same circumstances." According to Philip Zimbardo of Stanford Univer-sity and Zeno Franco of the Medical College of Wisconsin, the pres-ence of a "heroic imagination" can turn ordinary folks into heroes. Such an imagination enables us to "consider how we might engage in bravery" when the time comes to answer a challenge. Here are the steps that Zimbardo and Franco say are necessary to foster a heroic imagination:*

- Maintain a vigilant mind-set to determine if heroic action is needed for situations you encounter.
- Learn to endure controversy and stand firm for your principles.
- Imagine what might happen if you do or don't take action.
- Resist the rationalization of inaction.
- Do not condone bad means because they may lead to good ends.
- Trust that people will eventually recognize your heroic actions and transcend anticipating negative consequences.

The point is that heroes, mensches, and simply likable and trustworthy people are enchanting, and if you want to enchant others, you need to aspire to these attributes, too.

My Personal Story, by Tony Morgan

Tony Morgan is a pastor, author, and church consultant based in Atlanta, Georgia. In this personal story, he explains how a church taught him about trustworthiness and enchantment.

ONE OF THE MOST ENCHANTING EXPERIENCES OF MY LIFE TOOK place back in the early nineties. Friends of ours invited my wife and me on a trip to Chicago. Experiencing Chicago for the first time was pretty enchanting, but that's not what impacted us most by that visit. While we were there, we attended a service at Willow Creek Community Church.

As someone who grew up in a religious tradition that was . . . well . . . very traditional and extremely boring, I had no idea church could be relevant to

---

* Philip Zimbardo and Zeno Franco, "The Banality of Heroism," Greater Good, Fall/ Winter 2006-2007, http://greatergood.berkeley.edu/article/item/the_banality_ of_heroism.

my life. At Willow Creek, we engaged in an experience that included current music (no organ), video technology (no stained glass), a comfortable chair (no pews), and a message with life application (no yawning).

My experience at Willow Creek opened my eyes to the possibility that churches could teach the same biblical message but use different methods to reach new generations. Today this style of ministry is fairly commonplace. Until that Saturday night almost twenty years ago, I didn't think it was possible for a church to truly connect with people who were unchurched and outside the faith.

By deemphasizing the rules and ritual, I felt I was connecting with real people. Authenticity nurtured trust. Trust opened the door for outsiders, even those outside Willow Creek, to embrace Willow Creek.

Chapter 4

How to Prepare

Create like a god. Command like a king. Work like a slave.

—Constantine Brancusi

N ow that we've got likability and trustworthiness under control, we can address your cause (that is, your product, service, company, or idea). This chapter explains the qualities of a great cause as well as the groundwork and preparation necessary to make it successful.

Do Something Great

Don't get me wrong: Steve Jobs can enchant the shell off an egg without disturbing the yolk, but without a Macintosh, iPod, iPhone, or iPad, Steve wouldn't have anything to sell NeXt. When you combine his vision, his fulfillment of this vision (that is, the great Apple products), and his stage presence, he's unstoppable.

In a perfect world, you are so enchanting that your cause doesn't matter, and your cause is so enchanting that you don't matter. My goal is to help you achieve both. First, let's examine enchanting causes. More than twenty years ago, I came up with a list of qualities of a great product. I've revised it a few times, and it's served me well for all these years. Here it is:

- **Deep.** A deep cause has many features. It means you've anticipated what your customers will need as they move up the power curve. For example, Google is a one-stop source for your online needs, ranging from simple search to managing your e-mail and voicemail to aggregating RSS feeds to analyzing your Web site. The selection of its products is incredibly deep.

- **Intelligent.** An intelligent cause solves people's problems in smart ways. For example, suppose you have a teenage driver in your family, so you're concerned about his safety. Ford's MyKey product enables you to limit your car's speed and to set a maximum volume for the audio system. It also sounds an alarm if the driver isn't wearing a seatbelt while the car is in motion, provides early low-fuel warnings, and chimes at forty-five, fifty-five, and sixty-five miles per hour. This is just what you need if you're thinking of buying a Mustang GT500 and you have two teenage sons.

- **Complete.** A complete cause provides a great experience that includes service, support, and a string of enhancements. For example, the Lexus experience is more than the steel, leather, glass, and rubber. After-sales support is as much a part of owning a Lexus as the car itself. A Lexus is a *deep* car because of its capabilities, and it's also a *complete* car because of all the ancillary services surrounding it.

- **Empowering.** An empowering cause enables you to do old things better and to do new things you couldn't do at all. It makes you smarter, stronger, and more skilled. It increases your confidence and your ability to control your life. This feeling of empowerment is the essence of why people love their Macintoshes and often consider their computers an extension of themselves.

- **Elegant.** An elegant cause means someone cared about the user interface and experience. An elegant cause works with people. An inelegant cause fights people. Examples of elegance: Eames chair by Herman Miller, Airblade hand dryer from Dyson, Audi A5/S5.

Here's my Enchantment Hall of Fame to get your creativity flowing. Jot down your examples, too.

	Guy's	Yours
Car	1965 Ford Mustang	
Macintosh	IIci	
City	Istanbul, Turkey	
Airline	Virgin America	
Book	*If You Want to Write*, by Brenda Ueland	
Political leader	Nelson Mandela	
Actress	Queen Latifah	
Engineer	Steve Wozniak	
TV host	Mike Rowe	
Female blogger	Jenny Lawson, "The Bloggess"	
Male blogger	Robert Scoble	
Singer	Corinne Bailey Rae	
Parenting	Adopting children	
Architecture	Antoni Gaudí	
Clothes	Aloha shirts by Anne Namba	

In a nutshell, a cause that is deep, intelligent, complete, empowering, and elegant makes the process of enchanting people much easier. If you combine such a cause with a likable and trustworthy person, you've got it made.

Conduct a "Premortem"

In medicine, postmortem ("after death") examinations try to determine the cause of death. Pathologists conduct them for legal or educational purposes and to provide family members with closure by helping them understand why a loved one died.

Postmortems seldom occur after the death of products, services, or organizations, because there's no time or money to study something that's already dead, there's no one around to study what happened, and the employees who are around are angry and in denial. It's difficult, therefore, to do much or learn anything after a cause is dead.

Premortems, according to Gary Klein, author of *Sources of Power: How People Make Decisions,* are a better idea because they can help prevent death rather than explain it. This is how premortems work. The team assembles during the launch phase. The team leader asks everyone to assume the project failed and to come up with the reasons why the failure occurred—for example, a shortage of parts. The team then figures out ways to prevent these reasons from happening— for example, by finding second and third sources for parts.*

The goal of premortems is to prevent the potential problems in order to increase the likelihood of success. In this way, premortems can yield five benefits:

- Identification of problems in advance rather than after they occur.
- Reduction of the likelihood of premature embarkation.

---

* Gary Klein, "Performing a Project Premortem," *Harvard Business Review,* September 1, 2007, http://hbr.org/product/performing-a-project-premortem/an/ F0709A-PDF-ENG.

- More creative and organized approaches to the challenges the teams will face.
- Heightened sensitivity to early warning signs, since the team has already considered them.
- Participation by more team members because of the less political environment.

Asking team members to critique an ongoing project is ineffective because people don't like to attack the work of others and fear that criticism will label them as poor team players who aren't "with the program." These five benefits make premortems good investments of time and effort. They can help ensure success and make dreaded postmortems unnecessary.

Set Yourself Up for Success

Sometimes the best way to enchant people is to make it easy for them to go with your flow. Consider an experiment that I conducted at the end-of-season barbecue for my son's hockey team. I placed two trash cans next to each other. One had no cover, so people could throw

Trash can that changes behavior.

anything into it. The other had a cover with a six-inch diameter hole—the perfect size in which to drop cans and bottles. There were no oral or written requests to segregate and recycle the trash.

Twenty teenage boys and their parents attended the party. While the parents were good folks, making their kids segregate trash was not a high priority for them. I'd been on road trips with the boys, so I knew from firsthand experience that neatness and cleanliness were not team values, to put it mildly.

Backing up for a bit, we had had many parties at our house, and my system had consisted of an open trash can and a blue plastic recycling tub. Few people segregated their trash at these past events, so I would have to go through the cans to find the recyclables—talk about an inconvenient truth!

The results of my experiment with the lids amazed me: the trash can with the round hole was not only filled with bottles and cans, but there wasn't anything other than bottles and cans in it. This is logical— it would take a deviant (or goalie) to roll up paper plates, for example, in order to shove them into the hole. The round hole was the perfect trigger to get people to do what they should.

The trash can without the cover was the acid test. Would people make the effort to segregate their trash or take the easy way out? I went through this can to count, and there were five beer bottles in it. In other words, five parents were either callous or clueless (the boys were not drinking beer). Also, these bottles were at the bottom— perhaps before peer pressure kicked in.

Maybe I'm nuts, but this illustrates how you can change behavior— "enchant" might be a stretch—if you create smooth paths for people. Taken to the extreme, this can result in trickery and manipulation whereby people do something contrary to their best interests. But if your motives are pure and you make it easy to do the right thing, people will not disappoint you.

Make It Short, Simple, and Swallowable

> Life was simple before World War II. After that,
> we had systems.   —Grace Hopper

Allen Kay is the founder of Korey Kay & Partners, a New York ad agency, and a modern-day version of a character from the television show *Mad Men*. After 9/11, he wanted to help combat terrorism and, doing what ad men do, he came up with a slogan, "If you see something, say something."

IF YOU SEE SOMETHING, SAY SOMETHING. BE SUSPICIOUS OF ANYTHING UNATTENDED. Tell a cop, an MTA employee or call 1-888-NYC-SAFE.

His client was New York's Metropolitan Transportation Authority, so the slogan soon appeared in subways and on buses and trains. This poster is a great example of communicating a cause in an "easy to swallow, easy to follow" manner.* This kind of message enchants people because they can understand it and communicate it. (A Google search for Kay's phrase yielded approximately eight million matches in 2010.) Here are ways to make your cause easy to swallow, and, therefore, easy to follow:

---

* Kevin Dutton, "The Power to Persuade," *Scientific American Mind,* March–April 2010, 26.

- **Use tricolons.** A tricolon is a sentence containing three parts of equal length such as "Eye it, try it, buy it" (Chevrolet's slogan in the 1940s), "Be sincere, be brief, be seated" (Franklin Delano Roosevelt's advice to speakers), and "Location, location, location" (real-estate wisdom). The cadence of three words or phrases is powerful indeed.

- **Use metaphors.** Metaphors are figurative comparisons that convey the meaning of your cause. For example, Johnson & Johnson's ad for Band-Aids was "Say hello to your child's new bodyguard." The use of the word "bodyguard" conveyed that the product was strong and that your child was valuable.

- **Use similes.** Similes are comparisons of two things that are introduced with the word *like* or *as* but are not alike in most ways. For example, "Taking drugs is like playing with fire" or "Hockey is like war and ballet." These similes provide a familiar starting point to help people understand what you are communicating.

- **Keep it short.** Can you beat "Got milk?" or "Just do it" as slogans? Short phrases are memorable and repeatable. Here are guidelines for brevity for the most-used communication techniques:

  - **E-mail:** six sentences
  - **Video:** sixty seconds
  - **PowerPoint and Keynote:** ten slides
  - **Business plans:** twenty pages.

- **Stay positive.** Scare tactics are hard to swallow and can backfire. For example, a warning that "Twenty-five million people are killing themselves by smoking" could convince folks that smoking is OK because 25 million people do it. Paint a realistic picture of future goodness instead of trying to scare people.

- **Show respect.** Actions that insult people's intelligence seldom enchant. Television commercials for miracle weight loss, everlasting beauty, or instant wealth fit into this category. When you disrespect people, you get resentment, not action. Instead, make something great, communicate the facts, and let people decide for themselves.

Why do people create messages that are not short, simple, and swallowable? Two reasons: First, a committee got involved and group-groped the result. Second, people got overenthusiastic about the wonderfulness of their cause and lost touch with reality.

Practice restraint to control both of these factors. Less is not only more but also better when it comes to crafting your messages.

Remove the Fences

My wife's friend recommended we stay at a certain hotel in Paris, so I tried to book a room there. The hotel's Web site explained that there was a booking fee of €5.6 (approximately $7), which I thought was odd, but, hey, it's a French hotel.

I tried to make a reservation and learned that I had to pay the charge even though there were no rooms available. In other words, I

Booking request noted

A e-mail has just been sent to you with a recap of the booking request below.
This request has also been sent to the applicable property, and they will reply within 48 hours by e-mail only.

***** WARNING! THIS RESERVATION IS NOT CONFIRMED YET! *****

Mr Guy Kawasaki,

An answer to your booking request will be sent to you exclusively by email within a maximum of 2 days, you will then have to confirm your reservation.

Summary of your booking request:

Reference: JHZN7E
(GMT: 5/6/2010 9:51:15 PM)

Check In date	Check Out date	Number of nights
Sunday 23 May 2010	Friday 28 May 2010	5

1 Duplex Apartment	Sun 23MAY 538.00	Mon 24MAY 538.00	Tue 25MAY 538.00	Wed 26MAY 538.00	Thu 27MAY 538.00	2690.00
>> Booking fees (non refundable):						5.60

Total booking amount: **EUR 2695.60**

LODGING NAME AND ADDRESS

Duplex Apartment n° 1
person 1: Mr Kawasaki Guy
person 2: Mr Kawasaki Beth

Best Regards,

Legal notice

was charged $7 to *try* to make a $3,500 hotel reservation. We will never stay there now, because I will not pay for the privilege of making a hotel reservation.

Part of preparing your cause for launch is to eliminate fences like this one. This example is a financial fence, but mental fences exist, too. A body of psychology research on "cognitive fluency" postulates that people prefer things that are easy to think about. For example, Drake Bennett, a reporter for Boston.com, cited three applications of this theory:*

- The stocks of companies with easy-to-pronounce names outperform those with hard-to-pronounce names, according to Adam Alter of the New York University Stern School of Business.
- Norbert Schwarz of the University of Michigan found that people provided more honest answers on questionnaires that were printed in a more legible font.
- People believe that rhyming observations are more accurate than nonrhyming ones—for example, "Woes unite foes" versus "Woes unite enemies." Matthew McGlone of the University of Texas calls this the rhyme-as-reason effect.

Let's say you want to order a bottle of champagne. You've heard of, can remember, and can pronounce Cristal. How about a bottle of Veuve Clicquot Ponsardin instead? Maybe one factor that makes Cristal so popular is that it's an easy name to remember and pronounce—regardless of how it tastes.

Not convinced? Then consider the multi-billion-dollar Indian company called Tata. This name is easy to remember and pronounce, and it means "grandfather" in some Indian dialects. For many

---

* Drake Bennett, "Easy = True," *Boston Globe,* January 31, 2010, www.boston.com/ bostonglobe/ideas/articles/2010/01/31/easy_true.

people, the word "grandfather" connotes love, warmth, and caring. (In America, Tata is also a slang word for "breast," which is titillating, too.)

Brands with fluent names like Cristal, Tata, Under Armour, Lego, the Body Shop, Boots, Roots, and Fat Tire have removed speed bumps from our minds. You could take this a step further by choosing a name that is fluent and descriptive—for example, 24 Hour Fitness and 3 Day Blinds.

I would be remiss, however, if I did not tell you that Norbert Schwarz sees a positive role for disfluency. He believes that people may think that something less familiar is more innovative. In this case, people may consider a bottle of champagne that they've never heard of and cannot pronounce more exclusive and desirable.

Häagen-Dazs sure made this work. Two Polish immigrants, Reuben and Rose Mattus, started the company in the Bronx. Today, the company is based in Oakland, California. The name is not from any Scandinavian language, but it sure sounds like an innovative and tasty brand from some fjord in northern Europe.

Perhaps the lesson is to remove speed bumps to take people straight to adopting well-known products and services from well-known companies—for example, iPhone from Apple. If you want people to notice differences from well-known products and services, however, you should use an unusual name like Häagen-Dazs, Amazon, or Zappos.

Provide a Default Option

One way to remove fences is to provide a default option. You see a default option in action, for example, when companies enroll employees in retirement plans. Because most people are lousy at saving money, it's often a good thing for employees to participate in this form of enforced savings.

To support this, the U.S. government has insulated companies against issues of investment appropriateness if they follow certain guidelines. Hence, most companies use an "opt-out" plan whereby people are enrolled unless they choose to remove themselves. Years later, people benefit from a decision that was made for them.

Award Accelerator

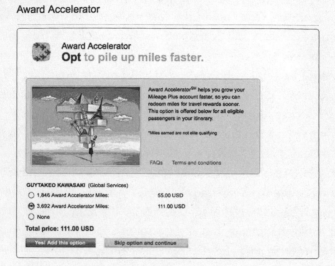

Defaults, though, can also irritate people. For example, when I made an online reservation with United Airlines, a screen popped up to ask if I wanted to buy miles to increase my points in the United loyalty program. The default was set to "Yes! Add this option," which leads people down a path they probably don't want to go. Much as I like United Airlines (I only noticed it because I buy so many United trips), this creeps into the zone of fooling gullible people and annoying others. Making the offer is fine, but United should not set the default to "Yes."

Establish Goals

"Would you tell me, please, which way I ought to go from here?"
"That depends a good deal on where you want to get to," said the Cat.

"I don't much care where—" said Alice.

"Then it doesn't matter which way you go," said the Cat.

—dialogue between Alice and the Cheshire Cat,

from *Alice's Adventures in Wonderland*, by Lewis Carroll

I won't urge you to establish goals for the usual management-guru reasons of measurability, communication, and leadership. My reason is that people who know what they want and can clearly explain their wishes are more enchanting. Etsy is an example of this. It is an online community of makers and buyers of handmade goods ranging from necklaces to baby clothes. It has hundreds of thousands of makers and even more buyers. Its goals are simple: "To enable people to make a living making things and to reconnect makers with buyers." Knowing what Etsy is trying to accomplish makes doing business easier for its makers, buyers, and partners.

By contrast, organizations that don't have goals or don't communicate them are more difficult to embrace, because their target audience is not sure what the organizations want. All they may succeed in doing is wasting people's time, and wasting time is disenchanting.

This principle may seem counterintuitive: How can I enchant people if I'm so blatant as to state my goals? First, this is the new, likable You 2.0 that has established likability and trustworthiness.

Second, stating your goals adds to the trust factor, because you are now transparent. Your agenda is on the table, and while people might not like it, at least they know what it is.

Create a Checklist

You can further systematize your goals by creating a checklist. But before I explain why checklists can help you enchant people, perhaps I can save your life by relaying a story about checklists in hospitals.

If you ever need a catheter line, try to remember the work of Dr. Peter Pronovost. He's a critical-care doctor at Johns Hopkins

Hospital, and he developed this simple checklist for medical staff to prevent infections from catheter lines:*

- Wash hands with soap.
- Clean the patient's skin with chlorhexidine antiseptic.
- Put sterile drapes over the entire patient.
- Wear a sterile mask, hat, gown, and gloves.
- Put a sterile dressing over the catheter site.

Pronovost asked the nurses in the Johns Hopkins intensive care unit to monitor if doctors followed this list. In a month, the nurses found that doctors skipped at least one step when treating more than 33 percent of the patients. Then he persuaded the hospital administration to allow nurses to stop doctors if they did not adhere to the list and to ask doctors every day if the catheter line was still necessary.

The results were dramatic: Line infections declined from 11 percent to 0 percent. In a fifteen-month period, the study showed that this checklist and the new role of nurses prevented forty-three infections and eight deaths and saved $2 million.†

Back to enchantment: A checklist is useful for three reasons. First, it helps people take action. With a list, there's a plan, and a plan focuses people on doing, not deciding what to do. (Remember, however, that rushing ahead prematurely is also dangerous, as I mentioned in the premortem discussion in chapter 4, "How to Prepare.")

Second, the existence of a checklist shows that you respect people's time and communicates that you know how to get things done. In short, it means you've got your act together. In a world of incompetent time wasters, people who have their act together are enchanting.

---

* Jane E. Brody, "A Basic Hospital To-Do List Saves Lives," Health (blog), *New York Times,* January 22, 2008, www.nytimes.com/2008/01/22/health/22brod.html?_r=1.
† Atul Gawande, "The Checklist," *New Yorker,* December 10, 2007, www.newyorker .com/reporting/2007/12/10/071210fa_fact_gawande.

Finally, a checklist motivates people because it enables them to see the progress they are making and feel a sense of accomplishment. This sense of accomplishment encourages them to do even more.

Here's a power tip from Steve Martin, the coauthor of *Yes!* A car wash offering a loyalty card nearly doubled customer retention by changing their offer from "Buy eight washes, get one free" to "Buy ten washes, get one free—and we'll start you off by crediting you for two washes."

So you might want to provide a checklist with the first few steps already checked off to increase its effectiveness.

My Personal Story, by Mike Stevens

Mike Stevens is a marketing consultant from Fargo, North Dakota, who helps printers improve their business. In his personal story, he explains how his dad rescued him from a lack of preparation when starting a business and how they built an enchanting business together. His lesson: If all your preparations fail (or you don't do any), there's always your family!

A FEW DAYS AFTER I BOUGHT MY LITTLE PRINT SHOP IN 1983, I realized I didn't have a clue what I was doing. I had a degree in business, but I quickly discovered my diploma was pretty much worthless in this new endeavor. On the second day we were open, a big snow blizzard hit our city, Fargo, North Dakota, and basically shut everything down.

I didn't have any extra cash and needed to be open because I needed the daily sales to make my first payroll in a few days. Somehow, I managed to get to work, thinking I could complete a few of the unfinished jobs in progress so I could invoice them for cash, but I quickly realized I didn't know how to operate a single piece of equipment.

The joy and excitement of owning a new business was fading fast. It felt hopeless. I did the only thing I could think of: I called my dad, who was a retired auto worker living in Florida. I said, "Dad, I'm lost. I don't know what to do or which way to turn." Without even pausing, he said not to worry, he'd be here in forty-eight hours. My dad got in his car and drove fifteen hundred miles—almost nonstop—until he got to Fargo.

When he arrived, the first thing he did was give me a hug and put his arm around my shoulder. (He'd never done that before.) I'll never forget him looking me in the eyes and saying, "It's gonna be OK, Mike. We'll get through this together, one problem at a time."

The next morning, when I got to work at five a.m., my dad was already there. He'd organized and cleaned things up and had breakfast waiting for me. I felt my anxieties begin to melt away. Soon, things did get better. Everyone loved my dad—especially customers. He became my front-counter person, my production manager, my delivery driver, and my inspiration. Sometimes it seemed like he did all the work and I got all the credit. But he wanted it that way. He became my secret weapon . . . and he ended up staying for twenty-three years.

During those twenty-three years, we worked together, we laughed together, and we learned the printing business together. In the end, my little business became a big success and won many printing industry awards. But I never forgot that my success was built on the shoulders of a loving dad who didn't want to see his son fail. He was always there for me, no matter what happened. I got my degree from the university, but it was my auto worker dad who taught me how to run a business.

He finally did retire at age seventy-seven. He died unexpectedly sixteen days later, at our family's little lake home that he was visiting on his way back to Florida.

In many ways, I'm not surprised. He probably planned it that way. After all, his job was finally complete.

Chapter 5
How to Launch

> There is no abstract art. You must always
> start with something. Afterward you can
> remove all traces of reality.
>
> —Pablo Picasso

H allelujah! You've created a kick-butt cause, and the next step is an epic, Helenic (as in "a thousand ships") launch—not the usual boring, limp, and anticlimactic spiel. This chapter explains how to tell a great story and immerse your audience in your cause to get it off to a fast start.

Tell a Story

> People don't want more information. They are up to their
> eyeballs in information. They want *faith*—faith in you, your
> goals, your success, in the story you tell.
>
> —Annette Simmons,
> author of *Whoever Tells the Best Story Wins*

I've watched product launches ranging from fully scripted, multimedia productions by famous CEOs to "two guys in a garage" using an old laptop. Most of these presentations follow the same pathetic script:

- Thank you for coming.
- We are introducing a patent-pending, curve-jumping, revolutionary new product today.
- This new product can slice and dice at a much lower price. Let me rattle off a list of vague features using incomprehensible acronyms.
- We'll introduce it soon, and we haven't set the final price yet.

Zero enchantment. Perhaps antienchantment, because people leave less intrigued than when they knew only rumors. Enchanting launches are more than press releases, data dumps, one-sided assertions, and boring sales pitches. They captivate people's interest and imagination by telling a compelling story.

Here are four story lines from Lois Kelly, author of *Beyond Buzz*, to help you craft a story that does your cause justice:*

- **Great aspirations.** Our heroes want to make the world a better place and know there must be a better way. Working nights and weekends, they create a better gizmo that people love more than their wildest dreams. Example: Steve Wozniak making it possible for more people to use computers.
- **David versus Goliath.** Goliath has a head start, incredible resources, and a cast of thousands. But young David whips out his secret weapon and defeats Goliath despite conventional wisdom that there's no way that he, the underdog, can succeed. Example: Southwest Airlines taking on the big airlines.
- **Profiles in courage.** Injustice, pain, and suffering are making our heroes' lives miserable. Despite these woes, they persevere and accomplish

---

* Guy Kawasaki, "The Nine Best Story Lines for Marketing," How to Change the World (blog), July 5, 2007, http://blog.guykawasaki.com/2007/07/what-people-tal.html#axzz10gqAZ7Rg.

great things. When you learn what they have done, your reaction is, "There's no way I could have done that." Example: Oskar and Emilie Schindler, the couple who protected Jews during World War II.

- **Personal stories.** "Epic" is not always necessary. "Illustrative" is enough—for example, personal stories like "My father owned a Cadillac, and he drove it 150,000 miles without major problems" are more effective than "This Caddy will last you a long time." Or, "I gave my teenage son an Android phone, and he told me he liked it better than his iPhone" versus "Android phones are good."

> It is faith that moves mountains, not facts. Facts do not give birth to faith. Faith needs a story to sustain it—a *meaningful* story that inspires belief in you and renews hope that your ideas do indeed offer what you promise. Genuine influence goes deeper than getting people to do what you want them to do. It means people pick up where you left off because they *believe*.
>
> **—Annette Simmons**

Immerse People

In San Diego, California, an organization called Strategic Operations provides what it calls a "hyper-realistic" simulation of battlefield conditions to train military personnel. The company is part of Stu Segall Productions, a TV and movie studio. It uses actors and special effects to create an immersive experience that swamps your knowledge that you're in San Diego, the guns are firing blanks, the flying shrapnel is cork, and injuries are only makeup.

I participated in an exercise at the company; my role was a U.S. diplomat visiting a village called Helmandi in Afghanistan's Pansar Valley. During a tour of the village, the enemy attacked us with an RPG, car bomb, and gunfire. My escorts rushed me out of harm's way. If you think Steve Jobs can make people suspend disbelief and think about what he's saying, you haven't had an RPG fired at you and run past a screaming soldier whose leg has been blown off.

Enrique Alvarez, one of the hyper-realistic actors at Strategic Operations.

The level beyond telling stories is immersing people in your cause. When you captivate people in this way, they lose track of time, suspend their cynicism and skepticism, and may also break into a sweat. Here's how to enable people to suspend disbelief without the Hollywood special effects:

- **Enable vicarious experiences.** A vicarious experience enables people to imagine using your cause via audio, video, or virtual reality technology. People lose themselves in the experience. For example, when you watch the guy at Blendtech shred an iPad, phone, or camera, don't you imagine yourself putting the gadget in the blender and flipping the switch?
- **Get as close to the real situation as possible.** The lesson of Strategic Operations is attention to detail. The company re-creates villages so that they look, feel, and smell like the real thing. Actors are in costume and speaking the local language. There are lambs hang-

ing in the shop windows. Amputees simulate soldiers whose legs have been blown off. When you pitch your cause, make the setting as realistic as possible.

- **Make a great demo.** Great enchanters give great demos. The key to a great demo is to show how a product works and how it enables people to do cool things. Using PowerPoint to list features and benefits is the antithesis of a great demo. You want people to imagine doing what you're doing in the demo, not wondering what your marketing dump means.

- **Anchor and twist.** "Anchor and twist" is the concept of Chip Heath, a professor at the Stanford Graduate School of Business, and Dan Heath, a senior fellow at Duke University. They are also coauthors of *Switch: How to Change Things When Change Is Hard.* Anchoring and twisting involves explaining your cause in terms of something familiar (anchoring) but then giving it a different meaning (twist).* This is a favorite technique of movie producers and book authors: "It's like *Dirty Harry* but set in the year 2100," or "It's *How to Win Friends and Influence People* brought up to date."

- **Differentiate from past experiences.** Immersing people requires something novel, quirky, and stylish. This doesn't mean you have to change their core beliefs; ideally, you'd reinforce core beliefs but move people to new manifestations of those beliefs. For example, "You've always wanted a fast car that doesn't ruin the environment. With our electric sports car, you can have both."

When you try to immerse people, ask yourself, "What would make me lose myself in the moment?" If you don't have connections at an organization like Strategic Operations, think of an immersive experience as a good amusement park ride: You don't think about anything except the ride while you're on it. That's the test—a hard one, but achievable nonetheless.

---

* Dan Heath and Chip Heath, "Selling Your Innovation: Anchor and Twist," *Fast Company*, July 1, 2008, www.fastcompany.com/magazine/127/made-to-stick-anchor-and-twist.html.

Promote Trial

Storytelling and immersion are effective ways to get people to consider embracing your cause. The next step is hands-on trial—so people can see for themselves. To enable hands-on trial, be sure to build these characteristics into the launch of your cause:

- **Easy.** *Easy* means people can try your cause without much training, guidance, expertise, or time. You want to appeal to their willingness to try something on a whim.
- **Immediate.** When people are hot to try your cause, let them proceed immediately. This means not requiring people to fill out long forms or wait for passwords and approvals to get started.
- **Inexpensive.** Ideally, the only cost for people trying your cause is their time. Few people will pay for the privilege of becoming a customer even if it's a highly recommended hotel in Paris.
- **Concrete.** At the end of a trial, people should observe concrete changes in the way they work or live their lives. They need to see results and effects to become believers.
- **Reversible.** If people try your cause and don't like it, they should be able to reverse their decision. Think of this as your Zappos's two-way, no-questions-asked, free-shipping return policy.

Amazon is an excellent example of how to promote trial. It does this in three ways with the books it sells: First, its "Look Inside!" feature enables readers to peer into books before they buy them. This mitigates the frustrating inability to browse through physical books. Second, readers can download sample pages of e-books prior to purchase. Third, people who bought Kindle e-books can return them, no questions asked, within twenty-four hours of purchase.

Prime the Pump

Adrian C. North, David J. Hargreaves, and Jennifer McKendrick of the University of Leicester devised a study to investigate the power of "priming the pump." The study, conducted in a market in the East Midlands area of the United Kingdom, involved displaying French wine and German wine while the market played French or German music near the shelf.*

The market sold forty bottles of French wine and eight bottles of German wine to French music. With German background music, it sold twenty-two bottles of German wine and twelve bottles of French wine. A questionnaire asked the shoppers if they were aware of outside influences as they shopped. When asked via an open-ended question, only one mentioned the music as an influence. When the questionnaire asked specifically whether the music was an influence, only six of forty-four subjects said it was.

The researchers interpreted these results to mean that music can "prime related knowledge and the selection of certain causes if they fit with that knowledge." So maybe the right music (or other environmental factors) can help you enchant people! And if you own a shop, you probably want to avoid playing "Shop Around" and "Walk On By" where customers can hear them.

Plant Many Seeds

Traditional marketing concentrates on "influentials" whom people recognize as experts. These influentials are journalists, A-list bloggers, analysts, industry gurus, and consultants. The theory is that if your cause pleases them, they will influence the great unwashed masses to adopt it.

---

* Tom Stafford, "Music, Wine, and Will," Mind Hacks (blog), February 6, 2006, http://mindhacks.com/2006/02/06/music-wine-and-will.

This is the old trickle-down, top-down theory that started when Moses went up the mountain to see God. Post-Internet, people have come to depend on the opinions of their friends and casual acquaintances as much as they do on experts, and this change has turned marketing upside down. (If you'd like to learn more about this approach to marketing, read the *Fast Company* article "Is the Tipping Point Toast?"* about Duncan Watts. He's the man behind this thinking.)

Now, when the masses adopt a cause, the influentials have to pay attention to it or risk looking clueless. Therefore, your enchantment efforts need not rely on influentials blessing your cause. Here's how to thrive in this new world:

- **Embrace the nobodies.** Lonelyboy15 and LATrixie are as likely to make your cause a success as A-list bloggers or traditional journalists. Anyone who understands and embraces your cause and wants to spread the word is worthy of your attention.
- **Give up the illusion of control.** Omniscience and omnipotence are illusions. You can't know who can and will help you. Nor can you control people you don't know. Sure, create the marketing, branding, and positioning that you hope will work best, but then let it rip and flow with the go.
- **Plant many seeds.** Think of this as "artificial dissemination." It involves planting fields of flowers, not flowerboxes. This is a strategy of big numbers: The more seeds, the more nobodies you'll reach, and the more likely they turn into somebodies for your cause.

There is an important difference between influentials and nobodies. Influentials are so busy acting influential that they often aren't power users of products. They try a product for a short time (or let an

---

* Clive Thompson, "Is the Tipping Point Toast?" *Fast Company*, January 28, 2008, www.fastcompany.com/magazine/122/is-the-tipping-point-toast.html.

intern use it), pronounce judgment, and then move on to the next shiny new thing.

Nobodies aren't similarly distracted. They have to use products in their jobs, so they understand what's needed and what's good (or bad). Nobodies, for example, decided Macintosh was good for desktop publishing. They also decided it wasn't good for spreadsheets, databases, and word processing.

Quality is more important than ever, because your product must pass more than the cursory examination of an influential. Still, the good news is that it's easier to reach nobodies, and any of them can become an oracle, so remember that nobodies are the new somebodies!

Ask People What They're Going to Do

In *Nudge: Improving Decisions About Health, Wealth, and Happiness,* Richard Thaler and Cass Sunstein explain that when you try to measure people's intent, you also affect their action. This is called the "mere measurement effect."*

The implication of this phenomenon is that you should ask people outright if they intend to support you. That's right: Ask them. Then you can reap three benefits:

- **You'll know where you stand.** This can help you revise your product and marketing early in the launch phase.
- **The act of asking can make people reach the tipping point and commit to you.** As an old boss of mine once said, "You don't get if you don't ask."
- **If people do commit to you, then they'll want to live up to their word.** (More on this in chapter 7: "How to Make Your Enchantment Endure.")

---

* Richard H. Thaler and Cass R. Sunstein, *Nudge: Improving Decisions About Health, Wealth, and Happiness,* (New York: Penguin Books, 2009), 71.

A simple follow-up can activate people who are sitting on the fence, so don't be afraid to ask. There's an old sales slogan that is still true: ABC (always be closing).

Reduce the Number of Choices

Sheena S. Iyengar, of Columbia University, and Mark R. Lepper, of Stanford University, showed that people are more likely to make a purchase when there are fewer choices.*

The researchers conducted the study at an upscale market called Draeger's in Menlo Park, California. (If you closed your eyes and threw baseballs in this market, you'd clobber venture capitalists and investment bankers, and the world would be a better place.) On two consecutive Saturdays, they arranged for shoppers to encounter a table displaying either six or twenty-four kinds of jam.

With six jams, 40 percent of passersby stopped at the table. With twenty-four, 60 percent stopped. This indicates that greater selection may increase initial interest. As measured by the redemption of coupons, however, 30 percent of passersby at the six-jam display and 3 percent of the passersby at the twenty-four-jam display made a purchase.

Moving from a study to the real world, a popular supermarket chain in Spain called Mercadona offers only two options for many products: its own house brand (Hacendado, "Landowner") and the most popular independent brand. The results of Draeger's study support this practice.

More choices can also lead to dissatisfaction because people may look back and wonder if another of the options would have been better. With more options available, there are more choices to regret. When it comes to analysis, perhaps more choices leads to paralysis, so fewer choices might help you enchant people.

---

* Sheena S. Iyengar and Mark R. Lepper, "When Choice Is Demotivating: Can One Desire Too Much of a Good Thing?" blog of Sheena S. Iyengar on Columbia University Web site, www.columbia.edu/~ss957/whenchoice.html.

Increase the Number of Choices

On the other hand, consider Miyo, a yogurt shop two blocks from Draeger's. Here customers can fill large bowls with any combination of fifteen flavors of yogurt (even guava) and then add sixty-nine different kinds of toppings (chocolate-covered almonds, bananas, strawberries, lychee, and even mochi).

The size of the bowl and the selection of toppings encourage you to create a concoction you'd never order from a server. The cost of the cup of goodness varies according to how much it weighs, so more is better for Miyo.

Picking out toppings at Miyo.

So what's the verdict: fewer choices or more choices? Maybe a decision is more significant with jam because you're committed to the bottle for a while, and greater selection makes the decision harder. The stakes are lower with a bowl of yogurt, so more choices aren't a hindrance. If you can, try both techniques, and let me know which works better for you.

Illustrate the Salient Point

Salient points take facts and use them to communicate the impact of a decision. For example, a label on a cheeseburger that says, "You'll gain half a pound by eating this" communicates more salient information than "Total calories: 1,500." More examples:

- **Cars:** miles per gallon versus cost of fuel per year
- **Heating:** thermostat settings in degrees versus heating expense per month
- **iPod:** gigabytes of storage capacity versus number of songs and movies the device can hold
- **Charities:** monetary amount versus how long your donation can feed a child

In each case, the first piece of information is only data. It requires additional information to provide meaning. The second piece of information explains an important factor at once. Put yourself in other people's shoes and ask, "Does this information help me make a decision?" The salient point of salient points is that they enable folks to make good, fast decisions, so provide this kind of information to the people you're trying to enchant.

Present the Big, Then the Small Choice

My eight-year-old daughter enchants me all the time. One of her favorite gambits is to ask me to take her to a local toy store called Cheeky Monkey. The store's owner has merchandised it for "helicopter" parents (so named because they hover around their kids) who don't spare any expense for their precious little jewels. Getting out of Cheeky Monkey, therefore, with less than a $20 purchase (a couple of Webkinzes) is Mission: Impossible.

When I say no to a Cheeky Monkey run, my daughter comes back with, "Then can we go to the candy store and get a treat?" I seldom say no to her. (Honestly, I don't anticipate saying no to her until she is married—and maybe not even then. And for sure I'll never deny her if she gives me grandchildren.)

With hindsight, I should not have used Robert Cialdini's book as a source of bedtime stories, because she's mastered what he calls the contrast principle. It means that after a big request for Cheeky Monkey toys, her request for candy seems reasonable by contrast, so I cannot refuse her.

As the television ads always say, "But wait, there's more" to the contrast principle. If you can get people to agree to small favors now, they are more likely to grant you big favors in the future. In 1966 Jonathan L. Freedman and Scott C. Fraser conducted a study in which they asked their subjects if they could enter their homes to catalog the household products they used. Only 28 percent agreed.

When they asked subjects to answer a few survey questions and then called back three days later to request entering their homes, 53 percent agreed. By getting their "foot in the door" with the small request to answer survey questions, the researchers doubled their success rate.*

Someone should do a study that combines both techniques: big choice, then small choice to get in the door, then big choice after having gotten in the door. That is, first, the researchers would ask the subjects for a big favor, such as entering the subjects' homes. Second, when most people declined, the researchers would ask for a small favor, "Then how about just answering a few survey questions?" Finally, after three days and having gotten their foot in the door, the researchers would again ask those who participated in the survey whether the researchers could enter the subjects' homes.

I just hope my daughter never learns the nuance of getting her foot in the door.

---

* Jonathan L. Freedman and Scott C. Fraser, "Compliance Without Pressure: The Foot-in-the-Door Technique," *Journal of Personality and Social Psychology* 4, 195–202, 1966.

Get Your First Follower

In 2010 Derek Sivers, the founder of CD Baby, showed a video at a TED (Technology, Entertainment, Design) conference. It started with one person dancing in a field. Then a second person joined in—validating the leader. Soon a third joined, and the crowd "tipped" into a full-scale dance festival.

The first follower jumps in and legitimizes the movement.

Sivers believes the first follower is important, because he brings credibility to the leader. Then, the subsequent followers emulate the first follower—not only the leader. In his words, "the first follower is what transforms the lone nut into a leader." The techniques we discussed in this chapter are geared toward attracting first followers, so now you are well equipped to go beyond the "lone nut" stage.

My Personal Story, by Matt Maurer

Matt Maurer is an entrepreneur and former venture capitalist in the San Francisco Bay Area. In his personal story, he explains how Vibram launched its unusual running shoe.

I CONSIDER MYSELF AN EXTREMELY SKEPTICAL CONSUMER, HAVING fully surrendered to a product only once in the last decade—to a pair of shoes, of all things.

It happened while I was chugging along through the park, nearly finished with a morning run, when another runner passed by in the opposite direction. He wore the strangest shoes—if you could call them shoes—which looked like a cross between a toe sock and a flip-flop. They didn't even cover the tops of his feet, and I could see each toe outlined in its own little pocket.

I thought back to a recent conversation with a friend about how we both preferred barefoot beach running to shoe-clad road running, and something just clicked in my mind. I actually pulled a one-eighty and ran this guy down—tapping him on the shoulder and giving him a start.

Apologizing, I asked about his shoes, and he launched excitedly into an explanation of something called the barefoot movement and theories about how traditional running shoes can sometimes oversupport a person's natural movements, altering the stride and increasing injury potential. At first, I just thought this guy had bought into some marketing gimmick, hook, line, and sinker; but as we talked, he revealed sound logic behind his theories and totally challenged what I thought I knew.

I was so intrigued that I searched everywhere for a pair to try on. No luck—apparently the company was shipping them in slow strategic waves, which made me resolve that if I found them anywhere, I would instantly pony up. Sure enough, two dozen calls later, I found a single pair at a runner's shop . . . in Ohio.

I don't know what captivated me more, counterintuitive claims against traditional shoes or the perceived scarcity of the product, but I know what sealed it—they actually worked. Not only did these things emulate barefoot running anywhere, but my come-and-go-again shin splints finally went for the last time.

In fact, speaking now as a full convert, I can say that the only feature of the Vibram Five Fingers that tends to hinder my running is the tendency for other runners to stop me and ask, "What on earth are you wearing?" or now, the more common, "Do those things actually work?"

Chapter 6

How to Overcome Resistance

To fly we have to have resistance.

—Maya Lin

First, the good news: You've launched your cause, and you're in the game. You even have some first followers. Next, the bad news: You now realize enchantment is a process, not an event, and "instant success" is an oxymoron. You will encounter reluctance, but people often resist anything worth doing. This chapter explains how to overcome resistance and get more people on board.

Why People Are Reluctant

In 1984, Nintendo of America was not a powerhouse game manufacturer. It went to the Consumer Electronics Show in Las Vegas with a product called Family Computer, or Famicon. By the end of 1984, Famicon was the bestselling game console in Japan, but efforts to market the Nintendo Entertainment System (NES), as Nintendo called it in America, failed.*

---

* GameSpy staff, "25 Smartest Moments in Gaming," Gamespy.com, July 21–25, 2003, http://archive.gamespy.com/articles/july03/25smartest/index22.shtml.

At the time, Americans thought the video game business was over. One reason was that the lousy Atari 2600 games had turned off American consumers. It was in these circumstances that Nintendo introduced the Robotic Operating Buddy, or R.O.B., for the NES. It was a gray, one-foot-tall robot with a light gun that spun on its axis, and only two games, Gyromite and Stack-Up, were compatible with it.

Nintendo used R.O.B., however, as more than a peripheral extension. The company used R.O.B. to position the NES as a toy, not a video game. Nintendo even created a television ad campaign that de-emphasized the use of a TV monitor to further reduce any video game association.

Kids fell right in line. They asked their parents for the Nintendo robot, not the Nintendo video game. They might have thrown in words like *science* and *educational*, too. The rest is history: Nintendo overcame the reluctance of retailers and parents and sold a million NES units in the first year and 3 million in the second year, making the product a huge success.

Enchantment requires understanding why people are reluctant to support your cause. In Nintendo's case, Americans had written off the video game segment. There are five common sources of resistance that you might encounter in similar circumstances:

- **Inertia.** Guy's law of enchantment: People at rest will remain at rest, and people in motion will remain moving in the same direction unless an outside enchanter acts upon them. Existing relationships, satisfaction with the status quo, laziness, and busyness hinder change.
- **Hesitation to reduce options.** People like, or at least think they like, the ability to make free choices and the availability of a breadth of choices (except, perhaps, when it comes to jam). Thus making a decision results in the reduction of options, and the prospect of this outcome can scare people.
- **Fear of making a mistake.** People may think that as long as they haven't made a choice, they haven't made a mistake. Once they

make a choice, they're either right or wrong. This fear of finding out can make people reluctant to make a choice—although not making a choice is itself a choice.

- **Lack of role models.** If there are no role models, people don't have behavior to copy, so they hesitate to give your cause a try. This is why early adopters are so important, as Derek Sivers illustrated with his video of people dancing in a field.

- **Your cause sucks!** There's no other way to put this: You or your cause may suck. Then people are right to be reluctant. God forbid that this is true, but it's often the case.

None of these factors is insurmountable unless your cause truly and permanently sucks. Resistance to change is the norm, not the exception. "Instant successes" are seldom instant, and if you talk to the people behind these successes, you'll find out that they came after months of fear, uncertainty, and confusion, along with a flagrant lack of adoption.

Provide Social Proof

Social proof is the concept that if other people are doing something, then it must be OK, right, cool, and maybe even optimal. Therefore, if you can show people that others are embracing your cause, you may convince them to embrace it, too. Here are three great examples of the power of social proof:

Example 1: One of Robert Cialdini's graduate students conducted an experiment at the Petrified Forest National Park in Arizona. The student placed two different signs on a trail and observed how the signs changed the rate of pilferage.[*]

One sign read, "Many past visitors have removed the petrified wood from the park, changing the natural state of the Petrified

---

[*] Noah J. Goldstein, Steve J. Martin, and Robert B. Cialdini, *Yes! 50 Scientifically Proven Ways to Be Persuasive* (New York: Free Press, 2008), 21–23.

Forest" and showed several people picking up petrified wood. The other sign read "Please don't remove the petrified wood from the park, in order to preserve the natural state of the Petrified Forest" and showed only one person picking up petrified wood.

When there was no sign, visitors took 2.92 percent of the marked petrified wood that experimenters had planted on the trail. When the sign depicted multiple visitors picking up wood, visitors took 7.92 percent of the marked wood—in other words, more pilferage occurred with the sign.

When the sign showed only one person picking up wood, visitors took only 1.67 percent of the marked wood. The implication is that people may infer that doing something wrong is OK if others are doing it, too. Showing them that few people are doing something wrong, however, has the desired effect.

Example 2: Families pay women to mourn at funerals in cultures all over the world. I posted a message on my blog asking for verification of this, and my readers told me this happens in Pakistan, Israel, Russia, India, Spain, Lebanon, China, Romania, Malaysia, Serbia, and Vietnam. In Vietnam, there are even two tiers of pricing: With and without tears!

These women provide social proof that the deceased was loved and will be missed. There's even a fable by Aesop about the practice:

> There was a rich man who had two daughters, but one of his daughters died. He hired some women to do the mourning, and they let loose a whole chorus of weeping. The other daughter remarked to her mother, "We are surely wretched women if we cannot come up with a lament for our own loss, while these women, who are not even members of the family, beat their breasts and grieve so deeply." The mother replied, "Don't be surprised, my child: they do it for the money!"

Example 3: Colleen Szot, a copywriter in the infomercial business, caused sales to increase when she changed the standard script from "Operators are waiting, please call now" to "If operators are busy, please call again." When people heard the new pitch, they concluded that the product was selling so well that operators couldn't keep up with incoming calls.*

After I learned about social proof, I altered one of my e-mail response templates. Whenever people wrote to me, I used to ask them to visit my Web site, Alltop.com. Then I pulled a Szot and added this line to my response: "If the site is slow or down, please keep trying, because we're getting slammed by traffic." At the time, we were, in fact, having scalability issues, but it's uncommon wisdom to portray this as a feature rather than a bug.

I wish I could tell you that this significantly increased traffic. The truth is that I don't know if it had any effect, because we were changing many variables at the same time. This is the difference between a well-designed scientific experiment and the real world of doing anything you can to improve results.

Create the Perception of Ubiquity

Social proof implies that when many people are doing something, it must be OK or the right thing to do. The "availability heuristic" is the related concept that the more easily you can think of an example, the more it is happening. For example, for each pair of ways of dying, pick the one that is more common:

- Murder or suicide?
- Shark attack or bee sting?
- Airplane crash or falling in bathtubs?
- Suicide, bee sting, and falling in bathtubs or unintended acceleration by a Toyota?

---

* Noah J. Goldstein, Steve J. Martin, and Robert B. Cialdini, *Yes! 50 Scientifically Proven Ways to Be Persuasive,* (New York: Free Press, 2008), 9–10.

The answer for each pair is the factor you've probably heard less about—specifically, suicides, bee stings, and falling in bathtubs cause far more deaths than, respectively, murder, sharks, and airplane crashes. Unintended Toyota acceleration might have caused forty deaths in ten years, but that's not what you'd think based on the news coverage of Toyota's woes in 2009–2010.

For most people, it's difficult to think of an example of deaths by suicide, bee sting, and falling in a bathtub, because the media seldom cover such events, and a long time will pass before there's a movie about a bee sting killing Brad Pitt while Angelina Jolie holds him in her arms.

In a more positive light, the white-corded headphones made it easy to spot people using iPods. Among the tech crowd, it was also easy to think of people who owned one. Hence iPods appeared to be ubiquitous, and this impression made them so. Is there anything more lovely than an upward spiral?

The bottom line is that familiarity breeds commitment, not contempt.

Create the Perception of Scarcity

At times the principles of social proof and ubiquity aren't feasible because of your price point (cars) or availability (art), but you still want people to desire what you provide. In that case, it's good to know that people assign more value to something they think is scarce. Here are three examples:

Example 1: When Google introduced its e-mail service, called Gmail, accounts were by invitation only. Do you think that Google had limited bandwidth or server space or that there were real reasons to limit the invitations? I don't. The desire for Gmail invites got so hysterical that people sold them on eBay.

Example 2: The illusion of scarcity is fundamental to the venture capital world of Silicon Valley. Here the only thing worse than investing in a bad deal is not getting in on a good deal. Craig Johnson, one of the godfathers of Silicon Valley corporate finance law, advised his young entrepreneur clients to tell potential investors, "The train is leaving the station, and there's not much room left," to get them to invest.

Example 3: My buddies in England run a chat Web site called XAT, where thousands of people communicate in chat sessions every month. The site sells "powers" that enable customization; for example, a power called Diamond adds a diamond-shaped background to the regular smiley.

When XAT offers a power, its customers buy several thousand in a matter of seconds. XAT withdraws the power when it stops selling, and then the price goes up in the aftermarket. Diamond initially sold for $1; a few months later, it sold for $10 in the aftermarket.

The illusion (or reality, for that matter) of scarcity is a barrier to fulfillment. Nevertheless, there are people who like to overcome barriers, so scarcity increases the buzz and desirability of your cause—for example, Matt Maurer's quest for a Vibram Five Fingers

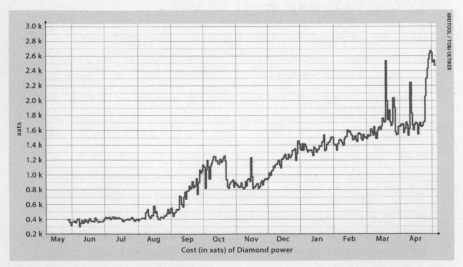

Cost (in xats) of Diamond power

Rise in price of virtual powers over time.

shoe at the end of chapter 5, "How to Launch." Also, if quantities are limited, then you can use this currency as a way to build bonds with your customers: "I'm doing something special for you by providing this."

One more good quality of scarcity: It encourages people to create a secondary market, such as the listings of Gmail invitations on eBay. These listings contributed to the perceived attractiveness of Gmail accounts when people learned folks were buying them on eBay.

Note: The past three sections provided recommendations that appear inconsistent if not downright conflicting: social proof and ubiquity or scarcity—what's it going to be?

The level of uncertainty and doubt determines which works best. For example, when people are uncertain or doubtful of your cause, use social proof and ubiquity methods to make them feel comfortable. When there's little uncertainty or doubt, then use the scarcity method to move them to action.

Or even better, you could use both: showing that something certain and accepted is also scarce.

Show People Your Magic

Waterford, the crystal maker in Dublin, Ireland, released more than one thousand craftsmen when it automated its manufacturing in 1987. Four years later, Denis Ryan convinced three of these laid-off employees to move to Nova Scotia to preserve their craft. They opened a factory and showroom in 1996 and called the company Nova Scotian Crystal. The factory and a showroom are near the ocean on the Halifax shore.

During warm weather, the company opens up a garage door to the street so people can peer into the factory and watch the craftsmen at work. Showroom educators use a public address system to explain what's going on. According to Rod McCulloch, the CEO of the business, enabling people to watch the manufacturing process "gets them into the showroom to buy eighty-dollar glasses."

Tourists watch the magic at Nova Scotian Crystal.

When people see how your magic works—manufacturing, brewing, cooking, designing—they develop an interest in what you do, and they are more likely to buy your products, support your idea, or join your cause. Factory tours and behind-the-scenes looks are all powerful enchantment tools.

Think about this: Do you know anyone who went on a winery tour who didn't conclude that the winery's products were good?

Find One Example

In November 2005, a sparrow flew into the Frisian Expo Centre in Leeuwarden, The Netherlands, a few days before the opening of Domino Day 2005. The naughty sparrow knocked down a few dominos that ended up tipping over 23,000 pieces. Fortunately, approximately four million dominos escaped being tipped over because of protective gaps in the structure.

The conference production company hired a firm named Duke Faunabeheer to capture the sparrow, but the firm did not succeed, so an employee shot the bird. When news got out, an animal-rights organization called Dierenbescherming sued Faunabeheer and the production company of the event. The public prosecutor fined the shooter €200 ($257) for killing a protected species.

Then news organizations and bloggers jumped into the fray. A radio disc jockey named Ruud de Wild offered a €3,000 ($3,900) reward for toppling all the dominos. Eventually there were death threats against Faunabeheer, the broadcasting company covering the event, and the production company. The Natuurhistorisch Museum in Rotterdam even exhibited the dead bird for seven months.

Millions of people have died in places like Rwanda and Darfur, and one has to wonder: Why do people go to extreme lengths to save an individual (and maybe a bird) and yet appear indifferent to genocides and mass murders? Paul Slovic of the University of Oregon studied this phenomenon. His conclusion is that the statistics of these mass tragedies "fail to convey the true meaning of such atrocities. The numbers fail to spark emotion or feeling and thus fail to motivate action."[*] Large numbers can overwhelm people: "I can't make a difference—it's too big a problem."

This means that less can be more when enchanting people. Slovic recommends several elements to move people to action rather than tuning out:

- **Use images.** Images are more powerful than words. A picture of a few people or even a single person can produce powerful and widespread emotions. For example, approximately 58,193 U.S. soldiers and up to 6 million Southeast Asians died in the Vietnam War, but this photo of Lieutenant Colonel Nguyen Ngoc Loan executing one Vietcong soldier came to represent the brutality of the conflict.

---

[*] Paul Slovic, "'If I Look at the Mass I Will Never Act': Psychic Numbing and Genocide," *Judgment and Decision Making* 2, no. 2 (April 2007), http://journal.sjdm .org/7303a/jdm7303a.htm.

It's surprising that Eddie Adams, the person who took the photo, did not intend it as a commentary on the Vietnam War. Years later he described what happened: "I thought absolutely nothing of it. I went back to the AP office, and I dropped it off. I said, 'I think I got some guy shooting somebody,' and I went to lunch." Remember Eddie's statement when you read chapter 12, "How to Resist Enchantment," where I discuss not falling for the example of one.

- **Illustrate the numbers.** In 1994, supporters of gun control arranged forty thousand pairs of shoes around the Reflecting Pool in Washington, D.C. The shoes represented the number of gunshot victims in the United States every year. At the time, Congress was considering gun-control legislation, and the pile of shoes provided a poignant and powerful way to illustrate the impact of guns in America.*

---

* Fox Butterfield, "'Silent March' on Guns Talks Loudly: 40,000 Pairs of Shoes, and All Empty," *New York Times*, September 21, 1994, www.nytimes.com/1994/09/21/us/silent-march-on-guns-talks-loudly-40000-pairs-of-shoes-and-all-empty.html.

• **Tell stories.** Personal narratives from individuals, such as *The Diary of Anne Frank* and Elie Wiesel's *Night,* communicated the true impact and meaning of the 6 million Jews killed during the Holocaust. Personal stories are powerful ways to make important events real and emotional to people.

Apply these elements to your efforts to enchant people for your cause, too. When you have a great example, one is not the loneliest number—it might be the most effective.

Find a Way to Agree

> Diplomacy is the art of letting someone have your way.
>
> —Daniele Varè

Once you find a way to agree, you are more likable, and when you're more likable, you're more likely to overcome resistance. After establishing a toehold, beachhead, or common ground, you can build from there, as these stories illustrate:

Story 1: France and Germany disagreed on policies, such as farming subsidies and trade regulations, but they did agree on the necessity of uniting Europe. Despite their differences, they helped to form the European Union.*

Story 2: Diplomats from two countries negotiated for a week with little progress until one stated he would have to return home in two days to attend the opera with his wife. A connection formed because the diplomats discovered they both hated opera and wanted to keep their wives happy. The tone of the negotiation completely changed after this discovery.†

Story 3: A father and his daughter didn't get along. He had no idea

---

* Hat tip to Chris Mooney for this story.

† Program on Negotiation Staff, "Small Talk, Big Gains," adapted from "The Final Word on Small Talk," Guhan Subramanian, www.pon.harvard.edu/daily/business-negotiations/small-talk-big-gains.

how to relate to her. One day she saw him packing the wheel bearings of his 1968 Ford Mustang. They got into a conversation about what he was doing, and she realized that working on the Mustang was a way to build a bridge to her father. From then on, they started to click.*

The point of these three stories is that if you look hard enough, you will often find something to agree on—even if it's agreeing to disagree. There's usually something—food, clothing, a football team, global warming, the latest clown who wants to be president of the United States, or disliking opera—to get you started.

Sure, you'd like an immediate and resounding agreement and a full speed ahead for your cause, but this isn't how the world works. Here are methods to find a way to agree:

- **Get personal.** Study her Web site, Flickr feed, Twitter feed, and blog. You might find something you both love—hockey, Audis, Van Gogh, or labradoodles. Perhaps you both have kids, so you can share parenting stories.

- **Get professional.** Use a business-networking site like LinkedIn to find out more about the person's professional background and people you both know. Maybe you were both sales reps for Procter & Gamble. Shame on you if you cannot find something job-related in common with the person.

- **Harmonize objections.** A good enchanter believes objections are a way of saying, "Not yet" or "Tell me more" as opposed to "No." For example, if someone objects that your cause is too expensive, harmonize this concern by explaining that you have a longer warranty, longer service life, and higher resale value.

- **Ask "What if . . . ?"** When you're making no progress with a person, ask, "What if we were to change this?" Asking a hypothetical question to see if he'd agree if you made changes is a great way to overcome resistance. For example, "Would you buy an iPhone if it

---

* Hat tip to Laura Butler for this story.

came from Verizon and not AT&T?" (I sure hope this example becomes dated soon.)

- **Move the window.** The Overton window is a political theory that holds that there is a "window," or range of policies, that people will accept. The range is: unthinkable-radical-acceptable-sensible-popular. The theory is that you can propose something less acceptable to move your idea into the acceptable window. For example, gun control advocates could propose an "unthinkable" ban on all guns to get Congress to accept a "radical" ban on automatic weapons.

The point of these methods is to find a way to agree on something—almost anything—that will give you a way to live another day and keep enchanting.

Find a Bright Spot

In 1990, Jerry Sternin went to Vietnam on behalf of Save the Children to fight malnutrition. He didn't speak Vietnamese, and he didn't have a budget to address the issues that most outsiders thought caused malnutrition: poor sanitation, poverty, and ignorance. According to Chip and Dan Heath, authors of *Switch*, the first action Sternin took was to recruit local mothers to weigh the children in the villages.*

He discovered kids who were healthy and set out to find out why they were the exceptions. After he eliminated families that were rich or influential, he learned that the mothers of healthy kids were adding shrimp, crabs, and sweet-potato greens to their bowls of plain rice.

Because of this insight, he started a program wherein mothers of healthy kids taught the mothers of malnourished kids to cook with

---

* Chip Heath and Dan Heath, *Switch: How to Change Things When Change Is Hard* (New York: Broadway Books, 2010), 27–32.

these ingredients. The program worked because Sternin didn't rely on American wisdom or American "shock and awe." Local people used local wisdom to help their neighbors. After six months, 65 percent of the children were better nourished in the Vietnamese village Sternin studied.

Sternin's experience provides an important lesson for overcoming resistance. Instead of thinking you have the answer and trying to implement it, you should shut up, back off, and find bright spots that are already working. The goal is to catalyze change, not get your own way.

Sternin's experience also validates my own experience at Apple. In 1984, we thought we had it all figured out: Macintosh was a spreadsheet, database, and word-processing machine. Wrong—it turned out that the bright spot that saved Macintosh was desktop publishing. Customers showed Apple this market—it wasn't our Cupertino-centric wisdom or insights. It was their local wisdom.

Assign a Label

> To put a complex argument in a few words: instead of the deviant motives leading to the deviant behavior, it is the other way around: the deviant behavior in time produces the deviant motivation.
> —**Howard S. Becker**

The concept behind labeling is that people will fulfill the prophecy of the labels applied to them. For example, in 1975, Richard L. Miller, Philip Brickman, and Diana Bolen divided students into three groups, and the students' teachers provided three different kinds of feedback:

- **Attribution:** You know the material well. You work really hard. You're trying hard. Keep at it.
- **Persuasion:** You should do well. You should be doing better.

- **Reinforcement:** I (the teacher) am proud of your work. I'm pleased with your progress. You're doing excellent.

The persuasion group showed the worst results—the persuasion group was the least persuaded! The reinforcement group was second. The attribution group—that is, the kids who were labeled as knowledgeable and hardworking—did the best.

Molson tried to make one label stick to another in a series of television commercials called "I am Canadian" that featured a young Canadian man dressed in a plaid shirt and jeans extolling what's great about living in Canada—you know: hockey, beavers, and tuques. The ad would close with "My name is Joe, and I am Canadian."

Applying a label that complements your cause can encourage people to embrace your enchantment. For example, if you've been labeled a Canadian (or you've labeled yourself a Canadian), then the Molson ad would make you think that you should drink Molson beer.

Use a Data Set to Change a Mind-Set

When it comes to presentations, Hans Rosling is the social activist, academic, Swedish version of Steve Jobs. Rosling is the professor of International Health at Karolinska Institutet and director of the Gapminder Foundation.

The Gapminder Foundation produces the Trendalyzer, a software application and Web site that transform statistics into dramatic and interactive graphs. Trendalyzer illustrates the power of using data to change people's minds. (Do yourself a favor and watch his TED presentations—just search online for "Hans Rosling.")

Here's an application of his work: People in Western countries believe that citizens of the Western world live long lives in small families, and citizens of developing countries live short lives in big families. In 1800 women in most countries had many children, as this graph, which plots the number of children per woman on the horizontal axis and life expectancy on the vertical axis, shows. Note that women in 1800 in the United States had more children than those in China and India.

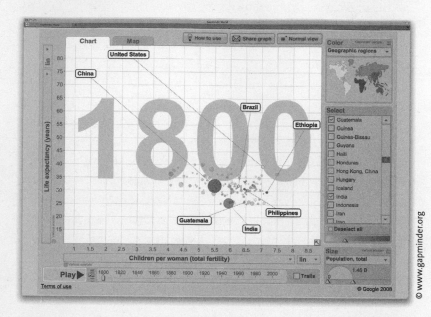

Rosling's software tracks the changes that occurred from 1800 to 2009. As you can see, most nations exhibit the common trend of fewer children per women and longer lives, and yet most people cling to old beliefs that woman in developing countries have many more children and much shorter lives.

Here's another example of using data. In 2003, the Dallas Museum of Art celebrated its hundredth anniversary by staying open for a hundred straight hours. The museum's management was surprised to learn that visits peaked from one a.m. to three a.m. This data persuaded the staff to rethink museum hours, and it instituted "Late Nights at the Dallas Museum of Art," whereby the museum stays open until midnight one Friday per month.

The work of Rosling and the experience of the Dallas Museum of

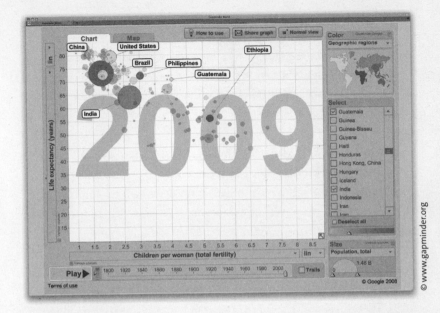

Art show that data sets are a powerful way to change people's mind-sets, so use them when the facts support your argument.

Incur a Debt

This story from *The Autobiography of Benjamin Franklin* illustrates the counterintuitive concept that asking people for help brings them closer to you. A new member of the General Assembly opposed Franklin's appointment to the prestigious and lucrative clerk position. Franklin explains how he won this person over:

> I did not, however, aim at gaining his favor by paying any servile respect to him, but, after some time, took this other method. Having heard that he had in his library a certain very scarce and curious book, I wrote a note to him, expressing my desire of perusing that book, and requesting he would do me the favor of lending it to me for a few days.

He sent it immediately, and I return'd it in about a week with another note, expressing strongly my sense of the favor. When we next met in the House, he spoke to me (which he had never done before), and with great civility; and he ever after manifested a readiness to serve me on all occasions, so that we became great friends, and our friendship continued to his death.*

According to Franklin, this illustrated an old maxim: "He that has once done you a kindness will be more ready to do you another, than he whom you yourself have obliged." There are two reasons for this:

First, once a person has helped you, he's more likely to help you again because refusing would mean he made a mistake in the first place. Assuming there were no bad consequences the first time, not continuing to help is to admit bad judgment.

Second, the prior interaction may have led to a better relationship. Therefore, doing something for you again has become natural. You, of course, should reciprocate, and an upward-spiraling, mutually enchanting bond can ensue.

So the thinking that people resent those who ask for favors may be wrong. Who are we to argue with Benjamin Franklin, anyway?

Enchant All the Influencers

When the Coast Guard Academy accepted a friend of mine named Rob Halsey, it sent a captain in full military dress to his high school to offer him the appointment. The academy understood that a student's peers and teachers influence his decision.

Many would-be enchanters define their targets too narrowly—that is, only the person who will adopt their cause. This often backfires because people don't make decisions by themselves. Think about the folks who may affect your decisions:

---

* Benjamin Franklin, *The Autobiography of Benjamin Franklin* (Philadelphia: Lippincott, 1868). Hat tip to Rich Mallon-Day for pointing me to this quote.

- Parents
- Grandparents
- Neighbors
- Pastors
- Teachers
- Coaches
- Spouse/significant other
- Friends (offline)
- Co-workers
- Facebook friends and Twitter followers

Consider this hypothetical situation. You are the CEO of a startup in any part of the world except Silicon Valley, and you are trying to enchant a great engineering student to leave the PhD program at Stanford to join your company, which you know is the "next Google." To make it harder, let's also say she's an overachieving Asian-American.

Unfortunately, her grandparents think she should finish her advanced degree so she can "always get a job at a big company." Her parents don't want to waste the tuition already spent, and they want to tell their friends that their daughter has a doctorate from Stanford. Her boyfriend doesn't want her to take the job because he knows she'll have to put in long hours. (My advice is to dump him if this is his attitude, but I digress.)

Here's a chart that explains how to enchant all the influencers:

Influencer	Concern	Response
Grandparents	Longevity of the company	"We have $10 million in venture capital in our bank account, and our board of directors includes the people who funded Google."

continued

| Parents | Wasted money on a degree not completed and the prestige of an advanced degree | "This real-life experience will make her education more relevant and valuable. Large companies love people who worked at startups and understand innovation. She can teach at Stanford after this experience. Worst case, she'll endow a chair at Stanford. Best case, she'll give a building." |
| Boyfriend | All-consuming work demands | "We believe a startup is a marathon, not a sprint, so we want our employees to have a balanced lifestyle." And if this doesn't work, "There are plenty of fish in the sea." |

Here are two more examples of enchanting all the influencers. First, Rhoda Davis of the Florida College Alabama Junior Camp held near Alexander City, Alabama, told me that kids are not her primary customers. Their sole priority is fun. Dad cares about the expense of the camp and that the kids return in one piece. The consumer Davis worries about the most is Mom. Mom's top priority is safety, and this is why you see several counselors in the pictures in the camp's brochure and on its Web site.

Second, the U.S. Navy had a problem recruiting young people because moms were against their kids' enlisting. The Navy hired a marketing firm called Campbell-Ewald to build a Web site called Navy for Moms. It is both for mothers with kids in the Navy and for mothers who have questions about Navy life. Within a year, the site had 27,000 members, 100,000 photographs, 750 videos, and 6,000 topics.

The data set showed that reluctant moms changed their minds

about the Navy on the eighth day of using the Web site. Over time, these moms each, on average, posted 4.2 photographs, responded to sixteen topics, watched eleven videos, and invited four other moms to join the Web site. The primary reason moms changed their minds was that they wanted to be proud of their kids.

It's naïve to think that you need to enchant only one person, so work on all the influencers. And great enchanters use the various influencers of a person to make their job easier. You may have to enchant a village, but the payoff is that the entire village can help you, because enchantment is often a collective experience.

Frame Thy Competition

If you're doing something worthwhile, you will encounter competition. In fact, if you don't encounter competition, you should wonder if you are doing something worthwhile enough. There are several ways to handle competition. At one extreme, you can attack it. This is counterproductive, inefficient, and downright silly.

At the other extreme, you can ignore your competition. This strategy can work if you feign ignoring them while you watch them closely, but it isn't the best you can do. The best way to handle the competition is a three-step process:

First, know thy competition. This means reading about them, trying their products, talking to their customers, and attending industry events. Because of the Internet, this is easier than ever.

Second, analyze thy competition. The best way to do this is to compile three lists of features and capabilities:

- What we both can do.
- What we can do but they cannot do.
- What we cannot do but they can do.

The beauty of this list is that it forces you to acknowledge the areas where your competition is superior to you. And if you cannot come up with ways the competition is superior to you, it means that you haven't looked hard enough or you are clueless.

Third, frame thy competition—paint as many rivals as possible into a corner with damning praise that will stick in people's minds. For example, in 2010, Steve Jobs framed Google when people complained that Apple excessively controlled the applications that ran on the iPhone, compared to the openness of Google's Android operating system.

He said, "Folks who want porn can buy an Android phone." In other words, he framed Android phones as the device for people who want to look at pornography. The Apple iPhone, by contrast, was a clean and controlled device for people who weren't perverts.

Control the Haptic Sensations

Haptic refers to the sense of touch and comes from the Greek word for "I fasten onto" or "I touch" (as opposed to iTouch). This is a little out there, but according to the research of Joshua M. Ackerman (Massachusetts Institute of Technology), Christopher C. Nocera (Harvard University), and John A. Bargh (Yale University), haptic sensations influence people's judgments and decisions.[*]

Specifically, these researchers found that using heavy clipboards produced impressions of importance and seriousness, handling rough puzzles makes social interactions more challenging, and sitting in hard chairs made people appear strict, stable, less emotional, and less flexible.

The theory is that simple tactile sensations influence higher-order feelings and judgments. So, for example, people sitting in soft chairs appear to be more flexible in negotiations. If this is true, it means you should hand people heavy clipboards and objects with smooth surfaces and stick them in soft chairs if you want to enchant them.

Hey, it's worth a try . . .

---

[*] Bill Hathaway, "Mind-Body Connection Is a Touchy Subject," *Futurity,* June 25, 2010, www.futurity.org/health-medicine/mind-body-connection-is-a-touchy-subject.

Remember Charlie

On June 3, 2010, Charlie Wedemeyer of Los Gatos, California, passed away from Lou Gehrig's disease (amyotrophic lateral sclerosis). This disease attacks the nerve cells of the central nervous system and traps its victims inside a body they cannot control.

Doctors diagnosed Wedemeyer's disease in 1978 when he was a high-school football coach and teacher. He continued to coach for eight years—eventually from a wheelchair with his wife, Lucy, reading the movement of his lips, eyes, and eyebrows to relay plays to the team.

For much of the rest of his life, he required 24/7 care. He breathed through a tracheostomy tube connected to a respirator and received nourishment through a stomach tube. Most people succumb to the disease in two years; Wedemeyer survived his medical marathon for thirty-two years.

After he stopped coaching, he continued to make appearances around the world, wrote a book, and inspired hundreds of young athletes. Hollywood made two movies about him and Lucy. He is the most inspirational person I've ever known, and Lucy is the second.

The Wedemeyers moved people with their passion and spirit even though Charlie could not move most of his muscles. The two of them provided guidance, inspiration, and *enchantment* to thousands of young people. Their story should inspire you when resistance is great and changing people's hearts, minds, and actions seems impossible.

My Personal Story, by Richard Fawal

Richard Fawal is the CEO of WatchParty in Austin, Texas. In his personal story, he explains how his resistance to using sticky notes as a planning tool was overcome.

IN THE 1980S, I WORKED FOR POLITICAL CAMPAIGNS. WE USED index cards with contact information, political precinct, and volunteering preference to keep track of supporters. We could only sort them one way at a time, so we spent hours re-sorting, and it was impossible to get a global view of volunteer assets.

One evening, a colleague arrived with packs of sticky notes in different colors, and I resisted: "What the hell are those for?" She wouldn't tell me, but she said she was going to solve all our problems. I was skeptical that little pieces of colored paper could help us. The next morning, I was amazed by what I saw.

On the walls hung dozens of ledger-sized pages. Each page had a precinct number written on it and was covered in different colored stickies containing supporters' names and contact information. The colors represented volunteer preferences.

With nothing but sticky notes, she had created a system to quickly find anyone we needed by name, precinct, or preference. It was a beautiful map that let us see where we were weak and strong, and which tasks were more and less popular. It changed the way I saw everything.

I used her system until computers made stickies obsolete a few years later. How I became enchanted by sticky notes is one of my favorite stories and a lesson I call upon every time I have a problem to solve.

Chapter 7
How to Make Enchantment Endure

I purchased my Tilley Hat at a fishing dock just south of the Everglades in Florida and thought the "hat" was rather expensive. Little did I know what I was buying would outlast the boat I was fishing in, the shoes on my feet, and now that I think of it, my marriage at the time. So I can safely say this "is" the best hat in the world. It loves to fish, doesn't complain about the hot sun or the cold rain, and when I get home, it doesn't care if I lay it down and ignore it the rest of the day. Yes sir, I've learned that you can count on a Tilley.

—David Halcomb (from the tag inside Tilley hats)

The goal of enchantment is a long-lasting change—not a onetime sale or transaction. In other words, you want enchantment to endure and, even better, to blossom. That's what happens when you change hearts, minds, and actions. This chapter explains how to get people to internalize your values and how to ensure that your enchantment lasts.

Strive for Internalization

In 1935, Lloyd Anderson couldn't find an ice axe he liked at a price he could afford. He ended up buying one from an Austrian store called Sporthaus Peterlong. Then he started helping his climbing buddies buy equipment from Europe. In 1938, he and twenty-one friends took their buying to the next level by contributing $1 each to form the Recreational Equipment Cooperative.

The firm is now called REI, and its 3.7 million customers shop at more than 100 stores. People go to REI not only to buy equipment but also to seek advice, socialize with folks who love the outdoors, and fantasize about where they can hike, bike, ski, and climb. REI has created an outdoors culture, and its customers have internalized REI's values.*

The process of internalizing values involves three stages: conformity, identification, and internalization. Here is an explanation of those stages:

- **Conformity.** People join because of peer pressure, coercion, trickery, or a desire to belong to a group. Conformity isn't enchantment and won't last long without undue force unless you move to identification and internalization.
- **Identification.** When people identify with members of a group, they see commonality and shared interests. No one is forcing them to conform. At this stage, the attractiveness of the enchanter and others in the group is important because people want the enchanter's approval.
- **Internalization.** This is the highest level. It means people have gone beyond identifying to believing. Their belief is not at odds with their feelings, there is no coercion, and they are not trying to please anyone. This is enchantment.

---

* Jay Greene, *Design Is How It Works: How the Smartest Companies Turn Products into Icons* (New York: Portfolio, 2010), 126–27.

Internalization is the hardest level to achieve, but the one that will last the longest. For example, I've internalized Macintosh. No one is coercing me to like it. (In twenty-seven years of using computers, I've only bought a Windows machine once, and I gave it to Goodwill long ago.)

I'm not using a Macintosh simply because I identify with other Macintosh users. I believe Macintosh is the best computer—so much so that I stand in line and pay the full retail price like any Apple customer.

Separate the Believers

> The people who are doing the work are the moving force behind the Macintosh. My job is to create a space for them, to clear out the rest of the organization and keep it at bay.
>
> —Steve Jobs

"Pluralistic ignorance" is the concept that people go along with something because they assume others agree with it. Pluralistic ignorance can then lead to "collective conservatism" or the unwillingness to change. Talk about a downward spiral!

To foster divergent thinking—or, more accurately, convergent thinking that's different from the predominant convergent thinking— it's necessary to separate believers from nonbelievers. Most new ideas don't stand a chance within the mainstream of an organization. This is why companies create independent business units for new products and services.

Thinking back to my Apple experience in the mid 1980s, Macintosh succeeded because the division was in a separate building with Steve Jobs leading it. Macintosh wouldn't have been born, much less succeeded, if it were in the center of a company focused on Apple IIs.

This leads to my theory that the optimal distance for believers from "headquarters" is half a mile—that is, too far for executives to walk to but still close enough to loot. As the tricolon goes: location, location, location.

Push Implementation Down

The traditional view of settling armed conflict involves bringing together the political and military leaders of the opposing forces. The assumption is that these leaders represent the broad constituencies of each side and can convince these people to support resolution.

Celia McKeon of Conciliation Resources, a charity organization that works to promote peace, disagrees. She believes that it is the grassroots members of communities who can most effectively "build trust and understanding," "assist in identifying and resolving local-level conflicts," and "create a safe, unofficial space for middle-ranking members of the conflicting parties to engage in problem-solving exercises in advance of negotiations."*

In other words, peace starts from the middle and bottom of societies, not at the top. For example, civil leaders helped bring about a lasting settlement in the border dispute between Peru and Ecuador in 1998. This settlement came out of a workshop at the University of Maryland called "Ecuador and Peru: Towards a Democratic and Cooperative Resolution Initiative."

The first workshop took place in 1997. Twenty members of the civilian populations of Ecuador and Peru formed the Grupo Maryland, and they worked to find a common ground for the resolution of armed conflict. Academics, businesspeople, educators, journalists, and environmentalists with "common traits related to profession, gender, age, location, and the like" made up the group.†

Grupo Maryland shows that to make enchantment last, you shouldn't focus on only leaders at the top. They have their own agendas—power, money, and self-image—that don't always reflect the entire population's desires, much less the greater good. The middles

---

* Celia McKeon, "Participating in Peace Processes," People Building Peace, www
 .peoplebuildingpeace.org/thestories/print.php?id=139&typ=theme.
† Inés Cevallos Breilh and Sahary Betancourt, "Grupo Maryland Between Peru and
 Eduador," People Building Peace, www.peoplebuildingpeace.org/thestories/
 print.php?id=144&typ=theme.

and bottoms of organizations are important, too—after all, that's who does the real work.

Use Intrinsic Methods

> I'm tired of hearing about money money, money, money, money.
> I just want to play the game, drink Pepsi, wear Reebok.
>
> —Shaquille O'Neal

Many people assume that money is the ultimate motivator, and this is not true. For example, think of all the volunteers who contribute thousands of hours to companies and nonprofit organizations.

Many organizations try to encourage people to help them by offering commissions and affiliate fees, but these enticements also raise suspicions (Are these folks spreading the word because they're getting paid?) and alter relationships (Am I spreading the word because I'm getting paid?).

Kathleen D. Vohs, a professor at the University of Minnesota, conducted a series of experiments to examine the effect of money on people's behavior. Here is a quick synopsis of three of her experiments:*

- Researchers provided subjects with $4,000, $200, or $0 in Monopoly money to play the game. As they left the lab, an accomplice of the experimenters dropped a bag of pencils, and the experimenters measured how many pencils the subjects picked up to help. The $4,000 subjects were the least helpful; the ones given no money were the most helpful, and the $200 subjects were in the middle.
- Researchers gave subjects eight quarters for unscrambling phrases into sentences. Some phrases dealt with money, and others

---

* Kathleen Vohs, "Small Steps, Big Leaps Briefing," Stanford University Graduate School of Business lecture series, February 12, 2010, www.youtube.com/watch?v=qrMoDJnJeF8.

didn't. At the conclusion of the experiment, subjects were asked for a donation to a student fund. The subjects who unscrambled phrases mentioning money donated less than those who unscrambled phrases that had nothing to do with money.

- Researchers placed subjects in a room with a computer that either had no screensaver, a screensaver depicting fish, or a screensaver depicting money. The researchers asked the subjects to set up two chairs for them to meet with other subjects. The ones who had seen the money screensaver set up chairs farther apart than the ones who had a blank screen or a fish screensaver.

These studies involved college students in a research project, so the results may not predict real-world results, but the students' actions indicate that exposing people to money affects their attitudes. Extrinsic rewards such as money are not necessarily effective enchanters.

An example of this is Wikipedia. Volunteers and amateurs created this vast information resource. No one paid them for their contributions to it. By contrast, Microsoft threw millions of dollars at Encarta, its online encyclopedia, but the project still failed. Microsoft reduced it to nothing more than an online dictionary in 2009.

It's not always true that you get what you pay for, and if you have a loser of a cause, money won't help. If you have a great cause, money won't matter. In practice, adding financial incentives to a great cause may hurt it, so think twice about using money as an enchantment tool.

Invoke Reciprocity

Invoking reciprocity is a powerful way to make enchantment last. Earlier, I told you how Ethiopia helped Mexico fifty years after Mexico helped Ethiopia. Here's another great story but at the city level.

Kids from the White Knoll Middle School in Columbia, South Carolina, presented a check for $447,265 to New York Mayor Rudy

Giuliani during the 2001 Macy's Thanksgiving Day parade. The students collected this money to enable New York to replace one of the fire trucks lost during the 9/11 attack. (Admittedly, the sum included one huge donation from a rich person.)

The kids from South Carolina reciprocated because, 134 years earlier, New Yorkers collected money to buy Columbia a fire wagon after the northerners learned that the city was using bucket brigades to fight fires. The first wagon sank on the way to Columbia, so the New Yorkers raised more money and sent a second one.

The generosity of the New Yorkers, many of whom were Union soldiers, overwhelmed a former Confederate colonel named Samuel Melton. On behalf of Columbia, he vowed to return the favor "should misfortune ever befall the Empire City." The kids made good on his promise 134 years later.

We discussed giving for intrinsic reasons in chapter 3, "How to Achieve Trustworthiness," but here is more information about the topic because it is so important:

- **Give with joy.** The purest form of giving is to those who cannot help you (for example, New York helping Columbia in the first few years after the Civil War) and without the expectation of return. Ironically, these gifts often catalyze the greatest reciprocation.
- **Give early.** "Pay it forward" by doing favors before you need favors back—if you ever need favors back at all. It's obvious and less powerful when there's a clear link between what you're doing and what you want back—that's a transaction, not a favor.
- **Give often and generously.** "As you sow, so shall you reap." If you give a lot, you'll also get a lot. If you give high-quality favors, you will get high-quality favors back, so do people favors that make a difference.
- **Give unexpectedly.** Richard Branson, the chairman of the Virgin Group, and I once spoke at the same conference in Moscow. I met him in the speaker's lounge, and he asked me if I ever flew on Virgin. I told him I didn't because I was a United Airlines customer. At

Richard Branson polishes my shoe and makes me a Virgin America customer for life.

that point, he got on his knees and gave me a shoeshine with his coat, and since then my first choice for any route that Virgin America flies is this airline.

- **Ask for reciprocation.** Don't hesitate to ask for a favor in return when you need it and the person you're asking can do it. This is a good practice because it relieves pressure on the recipient—you're providing a way to repay a debt. This enables the recipient to accept more favors, and your relationship can deepen.

Let me tell you my favorite Robert Cialdini story. I once sat next to him at a lunch at the Stanford Faculty Club, and we got into a discussion about what one should say when people thank you for doing them a favor. He told me that "I know you'd do the same for me" is a much better response than "You're welcome."

Cialdini's phrase tells the person who received your favor that someday you may need help too, and it also signals to the person that you believe she is honorable and someone who will reciprocate. If this is the spirit in which you're saying it, your response is far more enchanting than the perfunctory "You're welcome." On the other hand, simply trying to establish indebtedness isn't enchanting, so use the phrase wisely.

Catalyze Commitment and Consistency

Getting people to make a commitment to your cause and then invoking consistency in honoring it is a powerful way to make enchantment endure. Kanu Hawaii has put this concept in action. It's an organization of people living in Hawaii who love the state's unique culture and lifestyle. Members saw that environmental changes, increased cost of living, and fewer job opportunities threatened what they loved.

Kanu Hawaii encourages members to make commitments such as buying locally made products, cleaning up beaches, and adopting a green lifestyle. Sharing these commitments with friends and family via Facebook, Twitter, and e-mail is also central to Kanu Hawaii's philosophy.

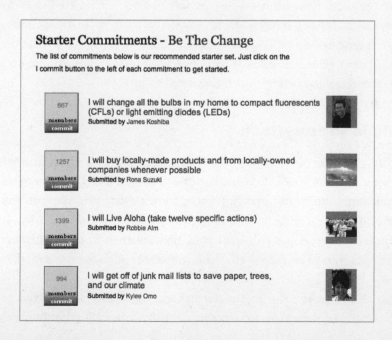

Commitment and consistency help enchantment endure on three levels. First, sticking to a commitment reduces the likelihood of people reconsidering past decisions and looking at all the options. There is a chance that people might not pick your cause the second time around.

Second, unless they lack a conscience, people like to honor their commitments. Your task is to show them why it makes sense to make a commitment in the first place. Then the desire for an honorable self-image enters the picture: "If I don't do what I said I'd do, it means I'm not an honorable person."

Third, telling others about a person's commitments creates another reason for him to honor them. Not fulfilling a commitment makes him appear to lack discipline or perseverance to his friends and family: "If I don't do what I said I'd do, it means others will think I'm not an honorable person."

Commitment and consistency can also work against you if people commit to your competition instead of you and want to remain consistent with their decision—for example, if you committed to Windows and refused to try a Macintosh. Nevertheless, I'm an optimist, so I recommend that you use the techniques we discussed in chapter 6, "How to Overcome Resistance" and then foster commitment and consistency to make your enchantment endure.

Build an Ecosystem

The presence of a community that complements a cause fosters endurance. Let's call this community an "ecosystem." It can increase the satisfaction that people receive from a cause and show to the world that you're successful enough to merit an ecosystem. Also, it means more people will help you, because their success is intertwined with yours. These are the components of an ecosystem:

- **User groups.** During the darkest moments of Apple's struggle to make Macintosh a success in the 1980s and 1990s, hundreds of

Macintosh fan(atic)s voluntarily ran user groups. These groups provided information, support, and enthusiasm to keep Macintosh going at times when Apple could not or would not. Many companies, such as Harley-Davidson, Oracle, Porsche, and Cisco have equally passionate user groups, too.

- **Web sites and blogs.** Enthusiasts, often consultants and developers in their off-hours, operate Web sites and blogs to provide information and support for the cause. Try searching Google for "WordPress blog" or "Windows blog" to see what I mean. The existence of these sites reassures both customers and potential customers of the value of causes. The sites also provide after-purchase support that increases satisfaction.

- **Consultants.** These folks develop expertise in helping others use causes. Therefore, they increase the satisfaction of customers. They have a vested interest in a cause's success because they can provide their services only as long as the cause continues to succeed.

- **Developers.** Whether it's a gaming box like Xbox, a computer operating system like Macintosh, or an online service like Twitter, developers are a huge reason for a platform's success and survival. These people create games, applications, and services that increase the utility of the platform and in turn increase the satisfaction people derive from a cause.

- **Resellers.** Stores and dealers who sell your wares are often the only entities that have a direct relationship with the consumer. They provide a convenient way for people to try, buy, and return your wares at stores like Best Buy. They can also provide consumer credibility—"Best Buy isn't going to stock a piece of junk." (Theoretically.)

- **Conferences.** You know you've arrived when you're big enough to hold a conference about your cause. Such conferences also signal to the world that you are big and successful. Most people believe that only the causes that have achieved critical mass can pull off such a gathering.

Now that you understand the key players in ecosystems, here's how to incite people to create or join your ecosystem:

- **Create something that's worthy of an ecosystem.** This is a constant theme of mine: The key to enchantment, evangelism, sales, presentations, and building an ecosystem is a great cause. In fact, if you create a great cause, you may not be able to prevent an ecosystem from forming. By contrast, it's hard to build an ecosystem around mundane and mediocre crap, no matter how hard you try.
- **Identify and recruit your evangelists.** If you have a great cause, find evangelists and ask them to build an ecosystem. (If you cannot find self-appointed evangelists for your cause, you may not have a great cause.) You may find that the act of asking these people to help flatters them so much that they sign up for duty, and you're off to the races.
- **Pick a champion for building the ecosystem.** Many employees may want to help build an ecosystem, but one person has to wake up every day with this task at the top of her priorities. Ecosystems need champions—identifiable heroes and inspiration—from within the company to carry the flag for the community.
- **Give people something meaningful to do.** People in your ecosystem aren't going to sit around composing love letters to your CEO about how great she is. Your believers need the ability to modify and improve the cause. In other words, you need an "open" architecture. For example, programmers can add plug-ins to Adobe Photoshop; motorcycle enthusiasts can customize their Harleys; and developers can make iPad apps.
- **Publish.** The natural complement of an open architecture is publishing books and articles about the cause. This spreads information to people on the periphery and can bring them into the ecosystem. Publishing also communicates to the world that your organization is open and willing to help external parties.

- **Welcome criticism.** Most organizations feel warm and fuzzy toward their ecosystem as long as the ecosystem says nice things, buys their products, and never complains. The minute the ecosystem says anything negative, however, organizations freak out and pull back their ecosystem efforts. This is dumb. A healthy ecosystem is a long-term relationship, so an organization shouldn't file for divorce at the first sign of marital discord. Indeed, the more an organization welcomes criticism and takes action to fix problems, the stronger its relationship with its ecosystem.

- **Foster discourse.** The definition of *discourse* is a "verbal exchange." The key word is *exchange*. Companies that want a healthy ecosystem should also participate in the exchange of ideas and opinions. At least your Web site should provide a forum where people can engage with other members as well as with the company's employees. This doesn't mean you let the ecosystem run your company, but you should listen to what members have to say.

- **Create a reward system.** You already know how I feel about paying people to help you, but this doesn't mean you shouldn't reward people in other ways. Simple things such as public recognition, badges, and awards have more impact than a few bucks. For example, Maker's Mark rewards its ambassadors (bourbon evangelists!) by putting their names on a Maker's Mark barrel and provides the opportunity to buy a bottle from the batch.

- **Publicize the existence of the ecosystem.** If you're going to all the trouble of supporting an ecosystem, you should make your ecosystem an integral part of your sales and marketing efforts. For example, the Harley Owners Group (HOG) (see below) is only one click away from the company's home page.

During the final testing of this book (yes, my books are tested like software), a reader commented that this ecosystem discussion related only to "high-tech, fairly big companies and thus, excluded me

and little players like me entirely." You know how I hate exclusionary models, so here are my thoughts about her issue.

First, the primary purposes of an ecosystem are to help you provide a better product or service and to establish credibility by demonstrating that the ecosystem exists. Any external party that does either of these is part of your "ecosystem." For example, a group of people advising you is a board of advisors, so right there you have the beginnings of an ecosystem.

Second, I hope you don't think that engineering geeks who started Silicon Valley's tech companies knew that they were creating behemoths. These companies started as "two guys/gals in a garage" and, to the surprise and delight of their founders, became huge successes with massive ecosystems. You might create the next billion-dollar company, so don't set any artificial limits. If you build an ecosystem (all ecosystems start small), you may become the next Google, Cisco, YouTube, or Microsoft.

Diversify the Team

A diverse team helps make enchantment last, because people with different backgrounds, perspectives, and skills keep a cause fresh and relevant. By contrast, when a naked emperor runs a kingdom of sycophants and clones, the cause moves toward mediocrity.

People of diverse ages, genders, races, economic standing, religions, cultures, marital status, household size, and educational backgrounds add richness and relevance to your efforts. In addition, you want people who offer various points of view within an organization:

- **Advocate.** The advocate takes the side of your customers, believers, and followers and proselytizes things like lower prices, faster delivery, free support, and more online engagement. She is the believer's champion inside the organization.
- **Skeptic.** The skeptic provides a doubting attitude to both positive and negative news. He challenges ideas to make them better. Do not confuse a skeptic with a cynic—a skeptic doubts, a cynic knows.
- **Visionary.** The visionary has a clear idea of how your technology and the marketplace will evolve. The visionary is often not the best manager, but you need someone to anticipate the needs of your believers before they can articulate these needs themselves.
- **Adult.** The adult makes things happen in an efficient, cost-effective, and legal manner. He complements the forward-looking visionary by checking the rear, side, above, and below views.
- **Evangelist.** The evangelist sells the dream of how your cause can make people's lives better. She uses emotion, intellect, and persuasion, but seldom money, to make people believe in your cause as much as you do.
- **Rainmaker.** The rainmaker closes deals. This role can involve selling ad space or convincing a foundation to donate money to your not-for-profit. People think making a sale is easy until they try to do it themselves.

Populating your organization with a diversity of people and capabilities, or at least people who can fulfill multiple roles, is a powerful way to make the enchantment last. There's no such thing as too much diversity in a cause that's staffed to last.

Promote Spreadability

The fans of the Grateful Dead, like the customers of REI, personify the internalization of values. For these fans, the Dead's appeal is their music plus a spiritual bond of friendship and growing up together. The band started in the 1960s and now has third- and fourth-generation fans—its enchantment has endured for a long time.

One reason for this longevity is that the band has supported the spreadability of its music. While the Recording Industry Association of America sues grandmothers for sharing music on peer-to-peer networks, the Grateful Dead encourages concert attendees to record its music and spread it.

Yes, you read that right.

According to David Meerman Scott and Brian Halligan in *Marketing Lessons from the Grateful Dead,* the band doesn't simply look the other way with respect to the "tapers" at concerts, it purposely allows them to set up professional-level equipment behind the band's own mixing equipment to assure good sound quality. And tapers can request seats in the special section reserved for them. There's even a section for tapers on the Grateful Dead Web site.*

The only limitation on the tapers is that they cannot use their recordings for commercial purposes. Other than that, they are free to spread the music. Over the years, the dissemination of music by

---

*. David Meerman Scott and Brian Halligan, *Marketing Lessons from the Grateful Dead: What Every Business Can Learn from the Most Iconic Band in History* (Hoboken, NJ: John Wiley, 2010), 105–7.

tapers succeeded in attracting more people to concerts and helping to sell more Grateful Dead music.

The Grateful Dead will probably endure long after bands with more restrictive rights have faded away because they encouraged people to enjoy their music freely.

My Personal Story, by Chris Anthony

Chris Anthony is a customer relations consultant in Richmond, Indiana. In his personal story, he explains how Disney enchanted him for life when a restaurant manager went above and beyond the call of duty.

WE WERE ON OUR HONEYMOON AT WALT DISNEY WORLD IN 2007, staying in a non-Disney hotel. The previous night, a member of the hotel staff attempted to break into our room. The management's response was, "You should have deadbolted the door." We were both shaken and scared all day; we barely saw the park we went to. Then we went to dinner at Jiko, in the Animal Kingdom Lodge.

While we waited, we told Sarah, the restaurant manager on duty, about what had happened. She asked us to wait and disappeared through a staff-only door. When she came back, she had room keys and said, "Cancel your rooms at the other hotel. We'll match its price for you here at the Animal Kingdom Lodge. That was unacceptable."

Our honeymoon could have been ruined by the offending staff member. Instead, Sarah, on behalf of Walt Disney World, turned it into something amazing. We've never forgotten—and we're never staying anywhere else.

Chapter 8

How to Use Push Technology

Because we do not understand the brain very well we are constantly tempted to use the latest technology as a model for trying to understand it. In my childhood we were always assured that the brain was a telephone switchboard. ("What else could it be?") I was amused to see that Sherrington, the great British neuroscientist, thought that the brain worked like a telegraph system. Freud often compared the brain to hydraulic and electro-magnetic systems. Leibniz compared it to a mill, and I am told some of the ancient Greeks thought the brain functions like a catapult. At present, obviously, the metaphor is the digital computer

—John R. Searle

This is a golden age of enchantment because reaching people around the world has never been easier, faster, or cheaper. Throughout the book I've mentioned how to use technology from time to time, but the next two chapters focus on the topic. This chapter explains how to use *push technology*—presentations, e-mail, and Twitter—to enchant people.

General Principles

What would Dale Carnegie do with Twitter? His book *How to Win Friends and Influence People* appeared in 1937. Since then, people have bought more than 15 million copies, and even now the book is one of the top two hundred bestsellers on Amazon. How cool is that?

Dale Carnegie would love Twitter. He would use it to reach his clients faster and more frequently. He would broaden his market by reaching people anywhere in the world with an Internet connection. Carnegie would also teach his clients to use Twitter to win friends and influence even more people.

How to Win Friends and Influence People continues to sell because it provides long-lasting principles. If Carnegie had based his book on the technology of 1937, I doubt people would still buy it. After all, in 1937 the average cost of a new car was $760; *Snow White and the Seven Dwarfs* was the most popular movie; and the BBC used an outdoor broadcasting unit for the first time (to televise the coronation of King George VI).

My hope is that *Enchantment* remains relevant for decades, too, so here is a list of general principles that should apply to technologies that I cannot foresee:

- **Engage fast.** When people contact you, respond fast. Fast, in 2011, means in less than a day. Few people respond quickly, and this is why they don't use technology as an effective enchantment tool. Luckily for you, this means a fast responder is unusual and therefore more enchanting.
- **Engage many.** Don't focus on the rich, famous, and traditional influential people. Treat everyone as equal and respond to as many as you can. You never know who will become your most valuable supporter and friend. Remember: Nobodies are the new somebodies in a world of wide-open communications.
- **Engage often.** Don't expect to engage people only a few times and be able to enchant them. Enchantment is a process, not an event.

You need to keep engaging—even when it seems there is little value in doing so. In the same way that few people engage fast, few people engage often, so it's also easy to stand out in this regard.

- **Use multiple media.** Generally, the more forms of media you use, the more enchanting you'll be. Text alone is so last century. Now there are pictures, video, live chats, and audio—and who knows what the future will have brought by the time you read this?

- **Provide value.** The main types of value are (1) pointers to useful, inspiring, or entertaining content; (2) personal insights, observations, or content; and (3) advice and assistance. When you find these gems, you should pass them along to your friends and followers to help them derive more value from online resources.

- **Give credit.** Credit whoever helped you find the valuable information that you provide to others. This is a "hat tip." Also, leave positive comments when you read something that you like. These actions are the equivalent of thank-you notes. The more you shine a light on others, the more you get noticed yourself.

- **Give people the benefit of the doubt.** Assume people are honest, smart, and decent—not dishonest, stupid, and conflicted. Don't lose your civility when you communicate digitally. And assume everything you do is public and permanent, so you are leaving fingerprints for anyone to see forever.

- **Accept diversity.** The broader and more flexible your outlook, the more enchanting your online presence. It's possible that you're wrong, or there are alternate explanations, methods, and perspectives. Agreeing to disagree is a viable philosophy. But there is a limit to accepting diversity, as my next point addresses.

- **Don't take any crap.** If you give people the benefit of the doubt and they violate you, don't tolerate it. My theory is that if you think someone is an asshole, most people who are silently observing the situation think so, too.

This is called Guy's Theory of Perfect Knowledge of Assholes (or *orifices,* if you prefer). If you don't take any crap, you will enchant the silent observers who like that you have the courage to push back. Just don't make your reaction personal; criticize the opinion, thinking, or perspective, but not the person.

- **Limit promotion.** Limit the amount of promotion that you do. Contrary to what social media fascists believe, the limit is not "none." If no more than 5 percent of your tweets, posts, and updates are promotional, you're doing OK. On the other hand, if no one complains, you're not promoting enough. As a rule, the more value you provide, the more you can promote your cause.

- **Disclose your conflicts.** I mentioned this in chapter 3, "How to Achieve Trustworthiness," but it's important enough to repeat: Disclose your conflicts. There are two reasons to do this: First, it's the honest thing to do. Second, if you have enchanted people, the causes you endorse will interest them. Therefore, disclosing your conflicts is good marketing.

These principles apply to everything except telepathy, time travel, thought control, and brain swaps. If such technologies become available, however, changing people's minds, hearts, and actions may not require enchantment, and people won't read this book anyway.

Presentations

> Speech is power: speech is to persuade,
> to convert, to compel. It is to bring another
> out of his bad sense into your good sense.
> —Ralph Waldo Emerson

Although I love general principles, I hate wimpy books that you put down (or is it "turn off"?) and find yourself asking, "But what do I do differently tomorrow?" The rest of this chapter provides action items and concrete suggestions for using technologies that exist in 2011. The first subject is presentations.

Al Gore tells his enchanting story.

If you think presentations cannot enchant people, you haven't seen a good one. Consider the impact of Al Gore's *An Inconvenient Truth*. In the course of an organization's life cycle, its management will have to give presentations to potential employees, customers, investors, advisors, vendors, partners, journalists, bloggers, regulators, and investment bankers (hopefully).

The most common presentation tools are PowerPoint and Keynote, although you don't need to use any technology at all. The key to a great presentation is a great cause. Assuming you do have something great, here are the keys to an enchanting presentation:

- **Customize the introduction.** Here's a secret: Great speakers give the same presentations over and over (how else can they perfect them?), but these speakers are so good that their audiences don't realize this. There is one part of a speech that you should change, however, and that is the beginning. Thus far I have not guaranteed anything in this book, but I guarantee that you will enchant your audience, at least for the first five minutes, by customizing your introductory remarks.

Think customized, not customary: "I'm so glad to be here today—blah blah blah." I use pictures to customize my speeches. For example, I showed pictures of all the Hewlett-Packard printers and faxes in my home and office when I spoke to the company's printer division. When I spoke to S. C. Johnson, I showed the audience pictures of the Pledge and Windex that were under our sinks. What do you think I showed when I spoke to Rubbermaid?

My best efforts happen when I speak in a foreign city. I usually get there a day early and tour the city to expand my horizons and to take pictures of what enchants me about it. If I don't have a chance to take a tour, then I photograph the audience and put them in my intro slides.

Here are examples of photos I've used in my speeches in cities around the world.

Standing with another sacred cow in Mumbai.

Learning about haggis at Crombie's in Edinburgh.

Checking out an elephant's foot at Bangalore Palace.

Giving Jesus a high-ten in Rio de Janeiro.

Measuring the size of Russian balls in Moscow.

Skating with Ken King, president of the Calgary Flames.

Trying on a fez in the Grand Bazaar, Istanbul.

Arm of an attendee at the Surf Industry Manufacturers Association conference.

- **Sell your dream.** Enchanters don't sell products, services, or companies. They don't think in terms of the cost of goods sold or glass, silicon, steel, leather, and rubber. Steve Jobs isn't thinking, *How can I get people to buy $188 worth of parts with a two-year contract from AT&T?*

  Enchanters sell their dreams for a better future—cooler social interactions, a cleaner environment, a heart-stirring driving experience, or the future of publishing. This perspective is the foundation for a presentation that transforms people. It makes them think of what could be, not what is. It enables enchanters to draw energy from the audience and then send it back at an even higher level.

- **Think screenplay, not speech.** Nancy Duarte of Duarte Design recommends you think of a presentation as a screenplay with three acts: Act 1 sets up the story and "what is." Act 2 presents the drama of "what could be." Act 3 resolves the story and explains

how to make it happen. There are more dull speeches than dull movies. Perhaps this is because speakers don't use a screenplay framework.

- **Dramatize.** Use evocative pictures, powerful videos, and sizzling product demos to make your presentation exciting. The goal is to provide inspiring information that moves people to action. And by the way, slides of text seldom enchant, so the fewer words on-screen, the better.

Steve Jobs and a minimal slide.

- **Shorten.** As a rule of thumb, the longer you need to pitch something, the less skillful you are, and the more mediocre the cause. My guideline is called the 10-20-30 rule: make a ten-slide presentation in twenty minutes with no font smaller than thirty points.
- **Practice.** Practice your presentation until you're sick of it. Then

practice it more. If you think Steve Jobs gets on stage and wings it, you're wrong. He spends hours preparing—and he's Steve Jobs. Imagine how much time the rest of us should practice.

- **Warm up the audience.** Go to the venue early so you can circulate with the audience. You'll reap two benefits by doing this: First, your confidence will increase because you'll make friends who want to see you succeed. Second, this interaction, no matter how brief, increases how much the audience supports you.
- **Speak a lot.** My last piece of advice is to make your presentation as many times as you can, because repetition improves the rhetorician. After the one-hundredth time, you may think that everyone who matters has already seen it. You'd be wrong. For example, Al Gore estimates he made the "Inconvenient Truth" presentation more than a thousand times.

Finally, if you have an hour to kill, watch the most enchanting speech I've ever given. It's from the Indus Entrepreneur conference in 2006, and all the forces of the universe lined up for me: high-energy crowd, standing room only, fans of my writing, and boring speakers preceded me. It wasn't so much that I was "on" as that the crowd turned me on. The culmination of the speech was when the crowd wanted me to keep talking even though the people running the conference tried to pull me off the stage.

E-mail

E-mail is the primary method of digital communication for millions of people. Maybe Facebook updates or other forms of social networking will replace it, but this will take a few years beyond the point at which I'm writing this book, so for the time being, mastering e-mail is still important. Here's how to use e-mail as a tool of enchantment:

- **Get a real e-mail address.** If you want people to take you seriously, your e-mail address should contain your organization's domain—as opposed to aol.com, gmail.com, or yahoo.com. Using such e-mail services is a signal that you're not fully dedicated to your cause, which will make people wonder why they should care about it.

- **Get an introduction.** The challenge of e-mail is to get people who don't know you, or their gatekeepers, to read it. The best way to do this is to get an introduction from someone the recipient knows, likes, and respects. Only the most dedicated people read e-mail that arrives over the transom without an introduction.

- **Personalize the subject line.** Even if someone introduces you to the recipient, the subject line is still important, because it helps people decide whether to read your message. If the recipient doesn't know you or hasn't been introduced to you, the subject line is critical.

  The kinds of subject lines that work include mentioning someone the recipient knows ("Your wife said to e-mail you"); providing an indication that the person is familiar with your interests ("Would you like to go to a Sharks game?") or your company ("Another news source for Alltop"); or sucking up in a great way ("I loved *Enchantment*").

- **Keep it to six sentences.** Of the hundreds of thousands of e-mails people have sent me, I cannot recall one that was too short. Ninety-five percent, by contrast, are too long. The ideal length is six sentences or fewer, and the message should contain no more than the following information: (1) why you're contacting the person (see "Suck up" below); (2) who you are; (3) what your cause is; (4) what you want; (5) why the recipient should help you; and (6) what the next step is.

- **Suck up.** A more politically correct way to say this is, "Do your homework," but the result is the same. Your first sentence should indicate that you are contacting the recipient for a good reason and that you know something about the person. For example, "I follow you on Twitter and notice you tweet about photography all the time. My company has developed a new way to help novices take better pictures."

- **Minimize attachments.** Attachments are an annoyance, and many people don't open them because they are afraid of viruses. For these reasons, you should seldom send attachments with your initial e-mail. If there's interest after the introduction, you can then ask the recipient for permission to send attachments.
- **Ask for something concrete.** If there's anything worse than an e-mail that asks for too much, it's an e-mail that asks for nothing—or is unclear about what the sender wants. If you have a person's interest and attention, do something with it. For example, ask the person to visit your Web site or to view a video. If your recipient is wondering what you want after reading your e-mail, you've wasted an opportunity.

Here is an example of an e-mail that worked on me. As soon as I got it, I installed the application on my iPhone. It's a little long, but the basics are there: suck up, explain what you do, prove you know what I'm interested in, and ask for something.

From: Priya Kane
Date: July 1, 2010 4:49:58 PDTPM
To: "guy@alltop.com" <guy@alltop.com>
Subject: iPhone/Droid App Review

Hi Guy,

My name is Priya Kane and I'm a representative from the indoor map company Micello. In a nutshell, Micello brings Google Maps to the indoors! We have made an iPhone/Android application that allows users to navigate through popular places such as airports, malls and schools using interactive maps.

In addition, Micello maps have unique features, such as a search bar to determine the location of buildings, point-to-point indoor navigation/ directions, and map "live feeds" to enhance user interaction.

At Micello, we have been following your blog posts for a couple months and understand that you have a large audience of viewers. Therefore, we wanted to inform you of our mapping application and were hoping you would check it out and possibly make a review for it.

We would love to hear your feedback on what you think of the application, and if you choose to make a review of the application that would be greatly appreciated. I can be contacted at micello.net if you need any further information.

Thank you,
Priya Kane
Micello
http://micello.net/

Twitter

Twitter is the most powerful enchantment tool I've used in my career. Its power exceeds that of Web sites and blogs because it is a push medium. This means people don't have to go to your blog or Web site to read your messages (tweets). Instead, all the people who follow your account on Twitter will see you post a message when they are using the service.

GET STARTED

To start, here are three ways to improve your use of the service:

- **Spruce up your photo.** Generally, men look better than their photo and women look worse, but most people should use a better picture. Physical attractiveness isn't necessary, but at least use a picture that's in focus and adequately lit. Make sure that your zygomatic major muscle (crow's-feet maker) is fired up. Here's a quick test: Double-click on your photo. Did it increase in size? Is it blurry? Are your eyes red?

- **Provide a descriptive profile.** The information in your profile is your business card, résumé, positioning statement, and pitch. Make sure that your profile provides all the information it can about your background, interests, and capabilities.

Guy Kawasaki

@GuyKawasaki Silicon Valley, California

Firehose that answers the question, What's interesting? Co-founder of Alltop. Former chief evangelist of Apple. Author of Enchantment.

http://www.facebook.com/enchantment

- **Repeat your tweets.** Some people disagree with me on this, but I repeat my tweets. I do this because Twitter is CNN, the *New York Times*, Reuters, and Associated Press on steroids all rolled into one. You should not assume that your followers will see your tweet if you post it only once, because they live in different time zones. This is the same reason CNN and ESPN repeat the same stories throughout the day.

POST INFORMATIVE LINKS

To enchant people with Twitter, you need to establish yourself as someone worth following by adding value to people's Twitter stream. There are at least three ways to do this: informational links, manual engagement, and marketing promotions.

britneyspears Britney Spears
@msleamichele NOBODY can help make a trip to the dentist a good time....- Britney
20 Oct

If you're a celebrity like Lance Armstrong, Britney Spears (see above), or Barack Obama, then tweeting that going to the dentist is a bummer might be sufficient. When it comes to most of us, however, nobody cares what show we're watching, how long the line at Starbucks is, or whether our cat rolled over.

nytimes The New York Times
Less Involved, Young Voters Say They Feel Abandoned
http://nyti.ms/9evBIT
1 hour ago

nytimes The New York Times
Our Towns: Spotlight in a Senate Race Won't Leave the Ring
http://nyti.ms/cil4tH
1 hour ago

nytimes The New York Times
Giants 4, Rangers 0: Rookie's Gem Has Giants on the Verge of a Title http://nyti.ms/bSMtlE
2 hours ago

nytimes The New York Times
Debt Collectors Face a Hazard: Writer's Cramp http://nyti.ms/bFTlzh
2 hours ago

nytimes The New York Times
For Donors, Vote Lays a Base for 2012 http://nyti.ms/9BDolV
3 hours ago

nytimes The New York Times
ImClone Ex-Chief Embarks on New Biotech Venture http://nyti.ms/baGFmZ
4 hours ago

Instead, post links that point people to stories, videos, and pictures they might not have found without you. The challenge is to find a large volume of links that appeal to your FFFs (friends, fans, and followers). Take it from someone who knows: Finding good content is hard work, so here are five methods to make it easier for you:

- **Push your own.** If you or your organization generates content for your Web site or blog, push this content out through Twitter. Organizations such as Mashable, CNN, and the *New York Times* (see below) tweet links to the content they generate. If you're in the business of generating content, this can work well for you.
- **StumbleUpon.** When you sign up for StumbleUpon, you tell it the subjects you're interested in. Then, when you "stumble," the service takes you to Web sites and blogs dealing with those subjects that other StumbleUpon users have liked. To get the most out of StumbleUpon, install the toolbar version into your browser. Like

VirginAmerica Virgin America
@ArielSacote Sorry about the gate change! Hope you were able to catch some Zzz's on your flight.
28 Oct

VirginAmerica Virgin America
@austinheap Thanks! Hope to have you onboard again soon!
28 Oct

VirginAmerica Virgin America
@RichCoulcher LAX or SFO -- your choice!
27 Oct

VirginAmerica Virgin America
Go on, Orlando. Give us a try. We'll make it worth your while. First-timers get 20% (+taxes/fees/restr) off here: http://vgn.am/6014HY2
27 Oct

VirginAmerica Virgin America
JFK weather is slowing down departure & arrival times today. Thx for ur patience. Pls check ur flight status here: http://vgn.am /6013Hct
27 Oct

approximately 14,846,969 people, I use the Firefox version because it lets me pick categories and share pages via Twitter, Facebook, and e-mail.

- **SmartBrief.** Smart people at this company sift through hundreds of stories to find the best ones for dozens of trade associations. The company then makes these digests available to anyone. All you have to do is go to its Web site or subscribe to its e-mail newsletters to benefit from their effort and expertise. You can think of SmartBrief as smart, human-powered news filters.

- **Alltop.** Imagine an online version of the magazine rack in a bookstore, except it has 850 subjects and is free. Alltop aggregates news by topics, presents the five most recent stories from the best Web sites and blogs about a subject, and gives you a preview of each story. There's no easier way to scan topics to stay current with the news. (Disclosure: I am the cofounder of Alltop.)

- **Interns.** You can hire people—usually interns—to find stuff for you. For $10 to $20 per hour, there are many eager, smart people who will comb the Internet to look for good content on your behalf. This is one of those times when throwing money at a problem can work.

The test for providing informative links is whether people find what you tweet so fascinating they forward it (retweet) to their followers. Truly, retweeting, not imitation, is the sincerest form of flattery these days.

ENGAGE PEOPLE MANUALLY

You can go far with broadcast-only informational links. Mashable, CNN, and the *New York Times* prove this because they are popular accounts to follow. Nevertheless, I haven't seen these Twitter accounts respond to people, so they're not as enchanting as they could be.

The reason organizations don't manually engage people is that it involves a lot of hard work, and it doesn't scale: How can they answer hundreds of thousands of followers? Not surprisingly, they're afraid of opening the floodgates: "If we start answering people, soon the volume will swamp us, and they will expect us to engage forever." They're right—this *would* happen. The question is whether the effort is worth it compared to other marketing expenses.

You can guess my answer: These days, Twitter is one of the cheapest and most effective ways to engage and enchant people. Companies like Virgin America (see below), Dell, Comcast, Ford, and Cisco answer questions and field complaints on Twitter, so you can do it, too, if you care enough and reap enough value from the efforts.

For example, Comcast supports engagement on both Twitter and Facebook with only ten people. At least give manual engagement a try—you could hire one less MBA, save $100,000 a year, and pay for two social-media staffers. You will find that nothing enchants people on Twitter like an organization responding to tweets.

PROMOTE YOUR CAUSE

The final kind of content is marketing promotions. You might recoil at the idea of this as content, but if you're looking for a deal on Dell

DellOutlet Dell Outlet
Last day of offer! Save up to 25% on select Dell Outlet Home PCs! (+ FREE 3-5 day shipping!) Get Your Coupons* here: http://del.ly /6012Ham
29 Oct

DellOutlet Dell Outlet
Last day of offer! Save 25% on any Latitude Laptop! Get Your Coupons* here: http://del.ly/6018Hai
29 Oct

DellOutlet Dell Outlet
No tricks, just treats! Online promotion happening now... save up to 25% on select Dell Outlet Home PCs! http://del.ly/6018Hjs
26 Oct

DellOutlet Dell Outlet
Check out our promo online at Dell Outlet Business... Save 25% on any Latitude Laptop! Get Your Coupons* here: http://del.ly /6019HnR
25 Oct

equipment (see below) or a Virgin America ticket, this kind of tweet is acceptable and even welcome.

You need to set your own parameters for using Twitter as a promotional mechanism, but 5 percent of your posts is a good target level for this kind of tweet. Notice in the screen shot of DellOutlet tweets that Dell is promoting its products as well as supporting its customers. This is a good example of using Twitter to sell and support.

MAKE IT PERSONAL

I saved my best Twitter tip for last: Take manual engagement to the extreme. Before you respond to people, look at their profiles so you can make your tweet more relevant. Few people make this kind of effort. Here's an example of what a highly personal exchange looks like. It starts with this tweet from me about a photo I found of my parents with John Wayne.

 GuyKawasaki Guy Kawasaki
Photo of my parents with John Wayne! http://om.ly/zOlk
1 hour ago

One of my followers responded with this tweet:

 SabineMcElrath Sabine McElrath
RT @GuyKawasaki: Photo of my parents with John Wayne!
http://om.ly/zMFn <~Your mother is stunning!
17 hours ago

I checked out her profile and learned she was a foodie.

 Sabine McElrath
@SabineMcElrath view full profile →
Maine

Coach, Social Media Consultant, Gourmande, Fanatic of all things Kitchen, Triumph Rider, Renaissance Soul http://www.smcurrent.com

This was my response to her response after I learned this:

GuyKawasaki Guy Kawasaki

@SabineMcElrath Why thanks for the kind words about my mother. BTW, have you seen http://food.alltop.com/?

17 hours ago

And this was her response to my personalized response:

SabineMcElrath Sabine McElrath

@GuyKawasaki My pleasure! Too much to explore on http://food.alltop.com/ I feel like a fruit fly drowning in a glass of pinot grigio!

6 hours ago ☆ Favorite ↻ Retweet ↩ Reply

Twitter has profile pages, and people fill them out. The information is there for you to engage people in the most personalized and enchanting ways.

My Personal Story, by Garr Reynolds

Garr Reynolds is an author and presentation consultant living in Nara, Japan. In this personal story, he explains his fascination with Japan and how the country has influenced his speeches and presentations.

I GREW UP IN A LARGE HOUSE RIGHT ON THE BEACH IN SEASIDE, ORE-gon. Our front yard had Japanese-inspired landscaping, including a koi pond and large stone lanterns. Once, while playing on the beach after a storm, I found a beautiful glass float that had broken loose from a Japanese fishing boat far offshore. I kept it in my room, as it reminded me of an exotic land on the other side of the Pacific, just outside my bedroom window.

In my twenties, I moved to Japan on an educational exchange program. I liked Japan immediately, but it took me three years before I truly adapted to the culture. In those early years, I took to studying the language and Japanese history as well as Zen and the many Zen arts such as sumi-e, tea ceremony, ikebana, Noh theatre, and so on.

Through experience and self-study, I shed my stereotypes and misconceptions about Japan and came to appreciate the depth and breadth of the culture and to see all the lessons that were there for anyone who was willing to learn. While I had a great time back in the United States when I returned, Japan kept calling me back—I was enchanted.

What is it about Japan? It is a mixture of many things. The food (*washoku*), for example, is as aesthetically beautiful as it is nutritious and delicious. Design and presentation matter. Customer service and respect for the "honorable customer" are unmatched anywhere in the world. And juxtapositions are everywhere: complexity and simplicity, modernity and traditional design, high-tech tools and ancient traditions.

Living abroad in general opens your mind and broadens your perspective. This is especially true in an ancient culture like Japan that embraces patience, cooperation, and humility. Japan has taught me to slow my busy mind, as I have learned the art of seeing things from another perspective.

My family is settled in a house we built in the quiet Nara countryside amidst Zen gardens, bamboo forests, Shinto shrines, and Buddhist temples. I am absolutely enchanted with the depth and breadth of Japanese culture and the lessons about design, economy, moderation, and living in harmony with the environment.

The traditional Japanese arts have taught me about the power of empty space and the importance of amplification through simplification and visual suggestion, and now I apply these lessons to presentations and book design.

The end of the following chapter contains more information about Garr's application of Japanese principles.

Chapter 9

How to Use Pull Technology

> The function of muscle is to pull and not to push,
> except in the case of the genitals and the tongue.
>
> —**Leonardo da Vinci**

Push technology brings your story to people. *Pull* technology brings people to your story. The advantage of pull technology is that you can provide large quantities of information—compared to, for example, the 140 characters in a tweet. This chapter explains how to pull people in and make the most of their attention when they visit your Web site, blog, and Facebook, LinkedIn, or YouTube pages.

Web Sites and Blogs

For distributing large quantities of information, selling your product, and providing support and downloads, it's tough to beat Web sites and blogs. Here's what you can do to maximize their enchantment power:

- **Provide good content.** This is a "duh-ism," but it's a duh-ism organizations miss. A Web site or blog without useful or entertaining content is not enchanting. This doesn't mean everyone has to like your content, but your site must appeal to the segment of the population you're trying to enchant.

- **Refresh it often.** Enchanting Web sites and blogs are not brochures that tell a marketing story and seldom change. Good content that doesn't change isn't good for long, and people will not return to your Web site or blog if you don't provide new material often. Ideally, you should update content every two to three days.

- **Skip the flash (and Flash).** You may think it's cool that a sixty-second video plays when people enter your Web site. Certainly your developer does. That makes two people in the world. Three, if you add the developer's mom. Skip the flash and Flash, and let people get right in unless you want them to abort their visit or only visit once.

- **Make it fast.** It's a shame when anyone can get right to your home page, but then has to wait for it to load. People expect immediate access, and there's no excuse for a Web site or blog that takes more than a few seconds to load.

- **Sprinkle graphics and pictures.** Graphics, pictures, and videos make a Web site or blog more interesting and enchanting. If you're going to err, use them too much rather than too little, with the exception of a Flash front-end intro.

- **Provide a Frequently Asked Questions (FAQ) page.** People love FAQs because FAQs cut to the chase. Figure out what the most common questions about your cause are and answer them in one place to save your visitors the hassle of searching for information.

- **Craft an About page.** Visitors should never have to wonder what your organization does and why you do what you do. Provide all this information in an About page. Confusion and ignorance are enemies of enchantment.

- **Help visitors navigate.** Enable people to search your Web site or blog to find what they are looking for. Also, a site map helps people understand the topology of your Web site.

- **Introduce the team.** Few people want to deal with a nameless, faceless, and soulless organization. A good Who Are We? page solves

this problem. Look at this great example from Arc90, a design shop from New York.

- **Optimize visits for various devices.** No matter what device people are using, your Web site and blog should look good. A Web site designed for a laptop or desktop computer isn't going to work well for a mobile phone or iPad, so create specific versions for whatever people use to access your site.

- **Provide multiple methods of access.** To each her own: Some folks like Web sites and blogs, and others prefer RSS feeds, e-mail lists, Facebook pages, and Twitter feeds. Provide multiple methods to engage people and make these options easy to find on your Web site.

A site that embodies most of these qualities is 1000 Awesome Things. This is how the creator of the site describes it:

My name is Neil Pasricha, and I'm a no-name thirty-year-old guy who started 1000 Awesome Things back in June 2008 with the goal of writing about one awesome thing every weekday.

I did this as my life was falling apart. My best friend took his own life, and my wife and I went different ways. We sold our house, I moved to a tiny apartment, and I tried to get things back on track by talking about one simple, universal little joy every single day—like snow days, bakery air, or popping Bubble Wrap.

Internet travelers from all over the world supported Awesome Things from the start and sent it to friends who sent it to friends. New people seeing the site helped us win the Best Blog award two years in a row and land a book deal.

This Spring *The Book of Awesome* comes out everywhere.

Honestly, this is just incredible, and I'm totally shocked and overwhelmed. But more than anything, I just want to say thanks.

The site features short descriptions of sweet little actions that make people smile—for example, when dinner guests do the dishes even though you told them not to, or when someone who doesn't like pizza crust gives their pizza crust to you. Take a look at the Web site's home page to see how such a page can help you enchant people.

Facebook

> I just use my muscles as a conversation piece, like someone walking a cheetah down Forty-second street.
>
> **—Arnold Schwarzenegger**

If Facebook were a country, by 2010 it would rank third in the world in population—behind China and India but larger than the United States. Enchanting Facebook members, therefore, is only reasonable and logical. When I was completing this book, I faced a choice between developing a Web page or a Facebook fan page for it. I picked the Facebook option for these reasons:

- Facebook's membership is large and contains the kind of people who would be interested in this book.
- The process of developing a Facebook fan page is fast, easy, and, therefore, inexpensive. I paid approximately $1,750 to a development company called HyperArts Web Design to create the fan page.
- The Facebook platform includes commenting, posting photos, posting videos, and sharing functionality. These features are all free.
- The Facebook platform supports third-party applications. If the Facebook platform can't do something, you can usually find an inexpensive or free application to do it.
- The identities of Facebook users are more reliable. For example, on a Web page, anyone can post a comment using any identity. When people post a comment on Facebook, they are much more likely to be the real person.
- The "liking" and sharing functionality of Facebook is fabulous.

This functionality enables people to spread the word about your cause. Once you enchant people with your fan page, you want them to spread the enchantment, too.

Mari Smith is the coauthor of *Facebook Marketing: An Hour a Day* and the lead author of *The Relationship Age*. *Fast Company* dubbed her "The Pied Piper of Facebook." I enlisted her expertise to explain how to use Facebook to enchant people. These are her favorite techniques:

- **Add a landing tab to your fan page.** An organization can specify which "tab" people see on its Facebook fan page. Most organizations call this their "Welcome" landing tab and customize it with graphics, promotional text, and sometimes a video message. The purpose of this tab is twofold: first, to provide first-time visitors a place to understand your Facebook presence and get oriented; second, to inspire visitors to join ("Like") the fan page and thereby help you spread it.

Facebook landing page for *Enchantment*.

- **Make use of Friend Lists.** To better manage your friends, create lists of important people. Then you can more easily view your News Feed each day and quickly "Like" and "Comment" to continue nurturing those important relationships.

- **Use your personal profile for professional networking.** Creating a personal profile allows you to reach out and add select individuals as friends, comment on their walls, and build key relationships. But control your status updates and posts because you never know who's reading your content in their stream.

- **Use @ tags strategically.** You can have up to six "@ tags" in any update/wall post (on your profile or fan page) consisting of a mix of friends, fan pages, events, or groups. Use @ tags to thank, acknowledge, and enchant people.

- **Provide an area for your fans to promote themselves.** To honor your fans and to minimize spam posts on your wall, give your fans their own forum with the Discussion tab. Specify how and where you want them to post. For example, Mari Smith has a long-running, popular thread encouraging fans to promote their Twitter accounts.

- **Respond to fans' posts promptly and personally.** Implement an effective engagement strategy (you may need team members to help) and reply to your fans' comments and questions. Personalize your replies and use fans' first names for an informal feel.

- **Surprise your fans.** From time to time, give your Facebook fan page a burst of excitement by introducing initiatives like "Fan Page Friday" or "Share Your Blog Day" and invite all your fans to share their links on your wall. Every wall post creates viral visibility for your page throughout Facebook!

- **Give special gifts.** Using the Facebook app on your fan page, you can add custom content as a tab or an item in the left column, including an opt-in box. Offer your fans a valuable, free download, and you'll grow your e-mail list as a result. Then you can continue building your relationship with your fans via e-mail.

- **Chat live with your fans.** Your fans will love to interact with you live from time to time. Use the Vpype or Ustream apps to stream live

video and get your fans to interact and chat. Also, try out the
Clobby app (Chat Lobby) to chat real-time with your fans. Your
fans will love you for the enchanting live element, and you'll
stand out from others on Facebook.

- **Get your fans involved in product and content creation.** Involve and
  include your Facebook fans when creating new products or when
  seeking ideas for new blog posts. This is called *crowdsourcing*. You
  can also run a contest. Wildfireapp.com is a good choice for con-
  tests on Facebook.

Facebook, with its membership exceeding the population of most
countries, is a powerful mechanism for enchantment. Despite its
size, Facebook requires personalized and informal, as opposed to
mass-marketing, techniques to enchant people. It's a weapon of
mass construction in the hands of a good enchanter.

LinkedIn

This is a simplification, but I could make the case that Facebook is for
show, and LinkedIn is for dough. This is because most people use
Facebook for socializing (although Mari Smith may singlehandedly
change this) and LinkedIn for making business connections or finding jobs. You may have to use both services to optimize your
enchantment efforts.

MAKE A GREAT PROFILE

The starting point of using LinkedIn as an enchantment tool is to
complete your profile. If you only enter basic information such as
your current employer and educational background, you're not using
LinkedIn to its fullest potential.

Completing your profile with all the key elements of your life
(education, work experience, affiliations, and activities) increases
your visibility, because LinkedIn will use this information to make
connections. (When I was writing this book, I reviewed my LinkedIn

profile and found that it was outdated! This is another lesson: Keep your profile current to maximize connections!)

GET VISIBLE

There are two additional ways to enable more people to find and connect with you. First, participate in activities at LinkedIn Answers. This is the section of LinkedIn where people ask and reply to questions. LinkedIn organizes the questions by topics, such as management, marketing and sales, technology, and international. Provide good answers, ask good questions, and you'll look like a star.

Second, LinkedIn's Groups directory contains thousands of special-interest groups. For example, there are over three hundred groups for event planners. Once you're in a group, participate in discussions to increase your visibility and get into the information flow of the group.

REACH OUT

So far I've focused on optimizing LinkedIn for pull functionality—that is, building your visibility and enabling people to find you. The other half of LinkedIn's value is enabling you to reach people, learn about their interests, check out their reputations, and get the inside scoop on organizations. Here's what I mean:

- **Search by name.** The simplest search is to enter a person's name. If he is on LinkedIn, you'll find his profile as well as people who are affiliated with him. You may already know some of these people, and LinkedIn will show you the people you both know. They might help you connect with him.
- **Search by company.** When you want to make a connection to a company but do not know anyone who works there, you can search for the company's name on LinkedIn and see the profiles of its employees. Then LinkedIn will show you the shared connections you have with the organization.
- **Find shared interests.** Once you find people on LinkedIn, you can learn about their interests and backgrounds—at least if they've

filled out their profiles. Knowing that you went to the same school, worked for the same company, play the same sports, or socialize with the same people is a powerful way to engage a person when you send an e-mail or meet for the first time.

- **Check the reputation of people.** Smart job candidates provide references from folks they know will say positive things, but you should get independent references, too. You can use LinkedIn to find people who worked at a company at the same time and ask them about job candidates. You can also use LinkedIn when you're considering a new position. Go to LinkedIn to find people who worked for your future boss and ask them if she's a good manager.

- **Scope out companies.** LinkedIn can provide information about trends at companies. For example, you may discover that most people in high positions at the company have MBAs from Harvard and went to Ivy League schools. LinkedIn can also reveal that employees are leaving a company to work for a competitor— so maybe you should consider that organization instead. Don't limit your use of LinkedIn to reach people and companies that you want to work for or sell to. You can also use it to scope out your competition, partners, and vendors. There's no such thing as knowing too much about all these types of organizations.

- **Integrate into a new job.** Here's a power tip to help you enchant people when you start a new job: Use LinkedIn to learn more about your fellow employees. It will help you build relationships much faster with people you don't know.

The bottom line is that LinkedIn is a tremendous enchantment tool because it enables you to find people, connect with them, find shared passions, and check their reputations.

YouTube

Greg Jarboe is the president and cofounder of SEO-PR and the author of *YouTube and Video Marketing: An Hour a Day.* In other words, he's the Mari Smith of YouTube (or Mari Smith is the Greg Jarboe of Face-book). I'm not an expert in YouTube, so I asked him to help me explain how to use it to enchant people.

PROVIDE INTRINSIC VALUE

The first thing Jarboe taught me is that video content that can enchant people must provide intrinsic value to your viewers. This value comes in four forms:

- **Inspiration.** YouTube has brought to light thousands of inspiring stories of courage and bravery. Example: "Jake Olson: A True Inspiration."
- **Entertainment.** Some videos are plain-and-simple guffawingly funny. Examples: "Re: @guykawasaki | Old Spice" and "*United Breaks Guitars.*"
- **Enlightenment.** These are documentaries similar to what you'd see on PBS or the Discovery Channel. Example: "Worse Than War | Full-length documentary | PBS."
- **Education.** Educational videos show how to do things and use products. Example: "How to Fold a T-shirt in 2 seconds."

(One way to remember these four categories is that they form the acronym "IEEE," which is funny in a nerd humor way. If you don't get it, don't worry.)

One important point: The goal of companies is often to create a "viral video." You know, the kind that millions of people watch in a few days—for example, the Old Spice guy videos. This is the kind of video every other company wishes it or its expensive agency created.

Don't make this your goal. Luck makes a video go viral, and "get lucky" is not a good strategy. The right goal is to provide a steady supply of video that is inspiring, entertaining, enlightening, or educational and that, over time, enchants people.

KEEP IT SHORT

The second thing Jarboe taught me is that the most popular videos are short. Despite its slogan, "Broadcast Yourself," YouTube isn't a broadcast medium. Instead, it's the world's most popular online video community.

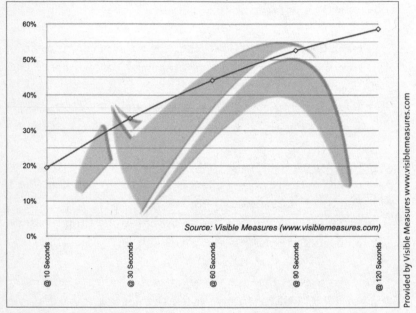

Source: Visible Measures (www.visiblemeasures.com)

Provided by Visible Measures www.visiblemeasures.com

Abandonment of videos over time.

In September 2010, my friends at Visible Measures analyzed over 40 million short (five minutes or less) video clips representing seven billion views. They found that 19.4 percent of viewers abandon a video within the first ten seconds. By sixty seconds, 44 percent have stopped watching.* Visible Measures' findings illustrate why enchant-

---

* Matt Cutler, "Benchmarking Viewer Abandonment in Online Video," Visible Measures Blog, September 29, 2010, http://corp.visiblemeasures.com/news-and-events/blog/bid/14410/Benchmarking-Viewer-Abandonment-in-Online-Video.

ing videos on YouTube are usually short. It's no wonder that popular videos such as "Charlie Bit My Finger—Again!" and "Evian Roller Babies" are only approximately a minute long.

The other key takeaway from these findings is that your videos should start fast because people are going to make a stop/continue decision in the first ten seconds. If you haven't enchanted them by then, you never will. So don't create videos that slowly build momentum and finally get interesting after a minute or so because many people will have stopped watching by then.

You can learn about your audience's viewing patterns by visiting the Insight tab. The reports there will show you how many views your videos are getting as well as viewer demographics. Documentaries are the exception to this rule, but the data set is clear: Ensure that your videos are short and sweet and start off with a bang.

FOSTER DISCOVERY, SHARING, AND IDENTITY

Assuming that you have IEEE content in a short format, next you need to accomplish three tasks to use YouTube to enchant people. First, help people discover your video. Did you know that the number of searches on YouTube is second only to that on Google? Here are three ways to make this work for you:

- **Keywords.** Relevant keywords can help get your video content in front of interested users. For help with choosing keywords, use the auto-fill suggestion drop-down menu on YouTube, study what other people have used as keywords for similar content, and use the same ones. Also, try YouTube's keyword suggestion tool. Finally, you can use the Discovery tab in YouTube Insight to access the keywords that people are searching to find your video.
- **Title, description, and tags.** After you've come up with new keyword ideas, ensure that your video includes those words within your title, description, and tags. This will help people discover your videos in search results and "Related Videos." If you want to

include your brand name in the title, it should always go last. Make your description and tags as detailed as possible.

- **Thumbnails.** Once YouTube has processed your video, it generates three representative video thumbnails. You can select one of them as your video thumbnail. As the Grail Knight tells Indiana Jones, "You must choose, but choose wisely." Think about which thumbnail is the most enchanting. Be aware that thumbnails that are sexual, violent, or graphic may cause YouTube to restrict access to your video.

Second, encourage people to share your videos as far and wide as possible. YouTube provides three powerful ways to make this happen: by embedding videos on other Web sites and blogs, by sharing links to videos via updates to services like Facebook and Twitter, and by e-mailing links to videos to people.

Third, build up a personal following and credibility on YouTube. Both of these will ensure that more people will watch your videos. You can accomplish this by leaving insightful, useful, or entertaining comments on other people's videos and joining YouTube groups. Increasing your visibility will attract people to your videos.

Finally, you can use Google Moderator on your YouTube channel. Moderator is a social platform that allows you to solicit ideas or questions on any topic, and your community can vote the best ones to the top in real time. Nick Kristof of the *New York Times* uses Moderator to take questions about his travels around the globe.

Think Japanese

Garr Reynolds's book, *Presentation Zen Design: Simple Design Principles and Techniques to Enhance Your Presentations*, contains a list of ten Japanese aesthetic principles. I'm sharing his list because this Japanese wisdom can help you increase the effectiveness of your use of technology.

Also, mentioning a few foreign phrases makes people think you're smart and more enchanting—and that's enough of a raison d'être to be part of your vocabulary.

- *Kanso.* Eliminating clutter and expressing things in plain and simple ways. Application: Reduce the crap in your presentation, on your Web site and blog, and in your e-mails, tweets, Facebook, and LinkedIn updates.
- *Fukinsei.* Using asymmetry or irregularity to achieve balance. Application: Use asymmetrical photos on your Web site and in your presentations. Google the "rule of thirds" to learn more about the power of asymmetry in photography.
- *Shibui.* Understating and not elaborating upon things. Application: Reduce the hard sell approach in every form of communication.
- *Shizen.* Depicting naturalness with the absence of pretense and artificiality. Application: Simplify the user interface of your Web properties and remove the flashy intro video on your Web site.
- *Yugen.* Using subtle and symbolic suggestion rather than obviousness. Application: Create a presentation that moves people's souls rather than beats them into submission and, more likely, boredom.
- *Datsuzoku.* Transcending habit, formula, and conventionality. Application: Break away from the tired text-and-bullet-points method of telling your story by using evocative pictures and cool diagrams. Or, don't use PowerPoint and Keynote at all.
- *Seijaku.* Achieving a state of tranquility and energized calm. Application: Remove the jarring and intrusive elements from your blog and Web site.
- *Wa.* Embodying harmony and balance and avoiding self-assertion. Application: Meld the needs of your customers, employees, and shareholders into a win-win, pie-baking approach.
- *Ma.* Providing an emptiness, spatial void, or silence to provide a focal point. Application: Remove the glitz from your slides and increase white space in your presentation, Web site, and blog.
- *Yohaku-no-bi.* Appreciating the beauty of what is implied, unstated, and unexpressed. Application: Don't sell past the close in your enchantment efforts.

And don't forget my contribution to Japanese concepts: *bull shii-take,* noun, the result of spreading lies, inaccuracies, and unfounded conclusions in a brazen manner.

My Personal Story, by Meryl K. Evans

Meryl K. Evans is a freelance writer from Plano, Texas. In this personal story, she explains how television (push technology!) with a closed-caption decoder opened up a whole new world of enchanting entertainment.

MY PARENTS NEVER HAD TO WORRY ABOUT ME WATCHING TOO much TV as a kid because I was born deaf, and I was unable to read lips on TV. I enjoyed cartoons and *Sesame Street,* but I played a lot of sports and stayed out of the house.

In 1983, I received a box bigger than two DVRs on top of each other. It was my first closed-caption decoder. No more than ten shows, if that, contained closed captions. It took work to find something where words appeared on the screen telling me who said what. Then I found Bond. I caught every one-liner and the bad guy's latest evil plan. No more asking my family "What did she say? What happened?"

Then I met the Carringtons. For the first time, I watched a weekly show experiencing the torture of waiting a whole week before finding out what happens next on *Dynasty.* One of my best friends was also a *Dynasty* fan. We had eighth-grade English together and we'd talk about the show. Wow—my first water cooler conversation around a TV show.

My parents also introduced me to musical theater. One year in June, I discovered something I never thought possible: the Tony Awards. Closed-captioned. At last, I could follow the words to the songs that I saw in the local theater. Thanks to closed-captioned Tony Awards and special programs like The Night of 100 Stars at the Palace, I learned many songs by heart because I could follow them on a music player.

Chapter 10

How to Enchant Your Employees

> To business that we love we rise betime,
> and go to't with delight.
>
> —**William Shakespeare**

H ere's another Japanese word: *bakatare*. It means "stupid" or "foolish," and it's the perfect description of people who think disenchanted employees can enchant customers. This chapter explains how to enchant the people who work for you so they can, in turn, enchant others.

Provide a MAP

Counterintuitive as this may seem, money is often not the sole, or even primary, reason for loving a job. Motivating people is not as simple as feeding money into employees and getting out results as if they were vending machines. Providing an opportunity for employees to achieve mastery, autonomy, and purpose (MAP) is more important than money.

- **Mastery.** People want to improve their skills and competency—true, maybe to make more money but also for the sake of getting better at something that interests them. Who wants to suck at something you do for eight hours a day?

- **Autonomy.** Autonomy means management isn't constantly telling people what to do and how to do it. When an organization enables people to work autonomously, this communicates management's belief that the employees are competent and trustworthy. So set the goals and get out of the way.

- **Purpose.** (This is the most important of the three factors, but MAP is a better acronym than PAM.) Purpose refers to the meaning an organization makes—in other words, how the organization is making the world a better place.

  FedEx's purpose is to give people peace of mind when they absolutely, positively need to get something somewhere. Target's purpose is to democratize design. eBay's purpose is to democratize commerce. Fulfilling a big purpose is a key element of employee satisfaction.

Providing meaning, autonomy, and purpose, however, doesn't mean that you should underpay people. If you underpay them, you are communicating that "We don't value you very much," so pay people a fair amount and enable them to achieve MAP, and you'll enchant your employees.

Empower Them to Do the Right Thing

> Rule #1—The customer is always right.
> Rule #2—When in doubt, refer back to Rule #1.
>
> **—House rules of Hyman's Seafood
> in Charleston, South Carolina**

Your best employees want to serve and delight your customers. This attitude expresses itself in the way great employees work—whether their task is to create something, manufacture it, ship it, sell it, support it, or revise it.

They care. A lot. Money isn't their sole motivation. The satisfaction of taking care of customers and making them happy is important, too. The bummer is that organizations don't let their employees do this. Unwittingly, they prevent employees from doing their best for customers with policies that are written to prevent losses, not achieve gains.

One easy way for you to enchant your employees is to empower them to do the right thing for the customer. This means you trust them to make responsible decisions (also known as autonomy) and to enable your organization to fulfill its reason for existence (also known as purpose).

On the other hand, if you don't enable your employees to please your customers, you create disenchantment. It means they cannot feel good about themselves, and you are putting them in the position of getting hammered by irate customers.

Bottom line: Let your employees do the right thing, and you'll enchant them. And then they will enchant your customers.

Judge Your Results and Others' Intentions

People often judge their *intentions* against the *results* of others: "I intended to meet my sales quota, but you missed yours." By doing this, they seldom find fault with their performance and almost always find shortcomings in the performance of others.

If you want to enchant employees, you should reverse this outlook: Judge yourself by what you've accomplished and others by what they intended. This means you are harsher on yourself than others and embrace an understanding attitude like "at least his intentions were good."

Over the long run, you cannot continue to judge people by their intentions if they consistently produce lousy results, but perhaps you made a hiring or training mistake. At least you should judge your results against the results of others and not give yourself the benefit of the doubt.

By the way, this is also very good advice for how you approach your results and your wife's intentions. The odds are very good that there are very good reasons for your wife's shortfall.

Address *Your* Shortcomings First

> So much of what we call management consists in making it difficult for people to work.
>
> **—Peter Drucker**

Continuing the theme of self-criticism, you should take active measures to find out what employees consider your shortcomings. Then start your performance reviews with employees by talking about how your foibles may have affected their performance.

Maybe your shortcomings caused the shortcomings of those who work for you. There's a saying that if a manager has to fire someone, maybe the company should fire him, too, because the situation should not have reached this point.

People who adopt this self-criticism strategy will improve as managers because they take responsibility for lousy outcomes. As important, they will inspire employees to improve through the good example that they set. Note: The word is "inspire" not "scare." Enchanted employees are inspired, not intimidated.

Think about this: How many performance reviews have you ever had where your boss started by saying, "I think I could have provided you with better management"? You will seldom go wrong blaming yourself first and most.

Suck It Up

The definition of *suck it up*, according to the Urban Dictionary, is "to endure a period of mental, physical, or emotional hardship with no complaining."* Sometimes you should suck it up and deal with

---

* www.urbandictionary.com/define.php?term=suck%20it%20up.

adversity, because that's what great people do. And as a bonus, you'll enchant the folks who work for you.

Stephen J. Cannell was the creator or co-creator of a number of television series, including *The Rockford Files, The A-Team, Wiseguy, 21 Jump Street, Silk Stalkings,* and *The Commish.* His story of how he worked with James Garner is the epitome of sucking it up:*

There were occasions when I sent a script down to him that I didn't think was the best script that we'd ever shot, and I'd never hear from him. A lot of other actors I worked with over the years would call me up and say, "Hey, I don't think this is a very good script, we need to do this, this, and this . . ." Never a word from Jim. Nothing. He'd just do it. So I started to think that he didn't see that it wasn't a good script.

Once we were at a wrap party at the end of a season, and one of those weak-sister scripts came up. Jim wagged a finger at me and said, "Not one of your better efforts, Steve."

So I said, "Okay, let me ask you a question: Why don't I ever hear from you when you don't like the script?"

He said, "I'll tell you exactly why: I trust you and I trust Juanita [Bartlett] and I trust David [Chase], and I know if you send me a script that isn't quite up to what we're used to doing, it's because it's the best you can do that week given the pressures that are on you. And if I spin you guys all around and force you to rewrite, I'm going to turn one bad script into four bad scripts.

"So that's the time that the acting department has to step up and really kick some ass. We have to step up and really make the stuff work. I have to look for more motivation to make comedy where I don't see it on the page and try to make it go past the audience without them seeing that it wasn't that good a story."

Whoa. I mean, come on. What a pro! What a pro! And he's

---

* Stephen J. Abramson, interviw of Stephen J. Cannell, Archive of American Television, June 23, 2004, www.emmytvlegends.org/interviews/people/stephen-j-cannell.

right: Very often I've found that when actors have spun me around like that—I know the script's not as good as it should be, but let's get past this one and have a good one next week. You can't do twenty-two excellent shows—it's just not possible. Anybody who does series television will tell you that. There's always a few that aren't as good.

He told me, at the same time, "You never sent me two bad ones in a row."

All I can say is *Capish?*

Don't Ask Employees to Do What You Wouldn't Do

If there is a single principle that can guide your management style, it is that you should never ask people to do something you wouldn't do. Nothing will increase your credibility and loyalty better than this.

Fill out this chart for a reality check.

Action	Do you?	Are you asking employees to?
Fly across the globe in coach class		
Answer all your e-mail		
Come in early and stay late		
Empty the trash can		
Make photocopies		

The point isn't that you should make every task fun—that's unrealistic. The point isn't even that you should do the grimy jobs. The point is that when you empathize with employees and work right alongside them, that's enchanting.

Celebrate Success

One win can overcome a hundred losses, so celebrating success is a powerful way to enchant employees. This is particularly true if you emphasize team wins rather than individual ones and give credit to all the employees involved. According to Brenda Bence, author of *How YOU Are Like Shampoo*, celebrating success has these positive effects:*

- It motivates your employees to work harder.
- It unifies the team around common goals.
- It uplifts employees' mind-sets from ongoing tasks to a celebration.
- It communicates the kind of goals the organization values.
- It builds momentum by illustrating that progress is happening.
- It reminds them that they work for a winning organization.

A cautionary word about celebrations: Good times tempt organizations to throw blowout bashes at expensive hotels with famous entertainers. This practice is a waste of money and a bad message to employees. The operative words are *fun* and *cool*, not *extravagant* and *awesome*.

The Industrial Extension Service of North Carolina State University provides a good example of an enchanting celebration of success. It aspired to create $1 billion of economic value for the region. When it achieved this goal, it celebrated by conducting a statewide bus tour of manufacturing companies. This is an example of a good celebration.

At each stop of the "Manufacturing Makes It Real" tour, NCSU people collected samples of products from the manufacturers and

---

* Brenda Bence, "Celebrate Team's Success and Boost Business," downloadable PDF, http://brendabence.com/media-room/articles/The-Top-10-Reasons.pdf.

"Manufacturing Makes It Real" on tour.

delivered these samples to the governor of the state. It was fun for the North Carolina State employees as well as rewarding for the employees of the companies that the bus visited.

Find a Devil's Advocate

First, a bit of history: From 1587 to 1983, the Catholic Church appointed people to argue against the canonization of particular individuals who were being considered for sainthood. The *advocatus diaboli,* or devil's advocate, role was to find fault with candidates to ensure saintly saints.

When the practice ended after the election of Pope John Paul II, an explosion in the number of canonizations occurred. During his reign the church canonized five hundred people, compared to ninety-eight during the reign of all his twentieth-century predecessors.

A devil's advocate to argue against canonizing company decisions and placing them above reproach can serve these valuable functions in your organization:

- **Improve your cause.** An organization needs to know what's going wrong in order to make it stronger. A stronger organization makes a better cause, and a better cause is more enchanting for employees (as well as customers).
- **Show that rocking the boat is acceptable.** The existence of a devil's advocate means that management is open to contrarian ideas and perspectives, and this fosters critical thinking among employees.
- **Foster internal communication.** A devil's advocate can serve as a focal point whom disenchanted employees can contact to discuss problems or grievances. His existence also shows that employees are free to discuss ideas that are often taboo in other organizations.

Any practice that improves your cause and your organization makes life better for your employees and enchants them, too—hence my advocacy for a devil's advocate.

Listen to Brother Bob

Bob Sutton is a professor at Stanford University and author of *Good Boss, Bad Boss: How to Be the Best . . . and Learn from the Worst.* He compiled a list of the twelve beliefs of good bosses. Think of it as the Good Boss Manifesto.

1. I have a flawed and incomplete understanding of what it feels like to work for me.
2. My success—and that of my people—depends largely on being the master of obvious and mundane things, not on magical, obscure, or breakthrough ideas or methods.

3. Having ambitious and well-defined goals is important, but it is useless to think about them much. My job is to focus on the small wins that enable my people to make a little progress every day.

4. One of the most important, and most difficult, parts of my job is to strike the delicate balance between being too assertive and not assertive enough.

5. My job is to serve as a human shield, to protect my people from external intrusions, distractions, and idiocy of every stripe—and to avoid imposing my own idiocy on them as well.

6. I strive to be confident enough to convince people that I am in charge, but humble enough to realize that I am often going to be wrong.

7. I aim to fight as if I am right, and listen as if I am wrong—and to teach my people to do the same thing.

8. One of the best tests of my leadership—and my organization—is "what happens after people make a mistake?"

9. Innovation is crucial to every team and organization. So my job is to encourage my people to generate and test all kinds of new ideas. But it is also my job to help them kill off all the bad ideas we generate, and most of the good ideas, too.

10. Bad is stronger than good. It is more important to eliminate the negative than to accentuate the positive.

11. How I do things is as important as what I do.

12. Because I wield power over others, I am at great risk of acting like an insensitive jerk—and not realizing it.*

This is a great checklist for people who want to determine how good (and enchanting) a boss they are. How many of these twelve characteristics do you embody?

---

* Bob Sutton, "12 Things Good Bosses Believe," The Conversation (blog) *Harvard Business Review,* May 28, 2010, http://blogs.hbr.org/cs/2010/05/12_things_that_good_bosses_bel.html.

Tell Them You Want Them

According to Michael Lopp, author of *Managing Humans: Biting and Humorous Tales of a Software Engineering Manager,* the three most important words that you should say during the recruitment process are "We want you."* He believes that once you've decided to hire a candidate, you should turn on the charm, communicate that you want him, have other employees take him out for drinks, and ask him for input before he starts.

I would extend Lopp's concept beyond the recruitment phase to every day whether the employee has worked for your organization for twenty hours or twenty years. When unemployment is high, you may think companies can scale back wooing their employees. This is wrong, however, because great people are always in short supply.

At the end of every day, one of the most valuable assets of your organization goes home. The question is whether they will return in the morning. An enchanting boss makes sure that her employees know they are valuable and they are appreciated. Remember the words "We want you."

How to Enchant Volunteers

Volunteers help organizations all over the world, and they are essential for the welfare and success of educational, environmental, social, religious, and other philanthropic causes. While the techniques already discussed in this chapter also pertain to volunteers, these folks deserve their own rules for enchantment:

- **Set ambitious goals.** Volunteers want to know that what they are doing is important and that they are making a difference. Your

---

* Michael Lopp, "Wanted," randsinrepose (blog), January 4, 2010, www.randsinrepose .com/archives/2010/01/04/wanted.html.

obligation is to set challenging goals and not waste their time. If there's anything worse than overusing volunteers, it's underusing them.

- **Manage them well.** When people believe, they want to help, and it's your responsibility to enable them to help as much as they can. This includes planning and organizing how you'll utilize their activities. You may not be paying them, but their time is still valuable.

- **Enable them to fulfill their needs.** Why do people join a nonprofit organization? There are three principal reasons: **duty** ("I should help my kid's school"), **belonging** ("I like doing things with people"), and **mastery** ("Learning a new skill is more important than money"). Fulfill these needs, and you're on the way to enchanting your volunteers.

- **Ensure that the paid staff appreciates them.** You and your employees must believe in the value of volunteers—if you lack this belief, maybe you should not recruit them. Volunteers often give their heart and soul to an organization, so it's important that your paid staff appreciates their efforts.

- **Give feedback.** People want to know how well they are doing. With volunteers, this is doubly important because you can't use compensation as a feedback mechanism. So after you set your ambitious goals, provide feedback, and they'll love you for helping them learn how they are progressing.

- **Provide recognition.** Recognition comes in small forms for volunteers: business cards, an e-mail address, a workspace (even if it's shared), attendance at conferences, and public and private expressions of gratitude. See anything that's expensive on this list? Good, because there isn't.

- **Invite them in.** At least once a year, invite your volunteers into your headquarters. This enables people to meet face-to-face instead of only virtually. Remember the value of proximity to achieving likability? The same concept applies to volunteers.

- **Provide free stuff.** "Stuff" means food and drink at working sessions as well as T-shirts and other forms of tchotchkes. Unfortunately, these kinds of goodies are often the first thing an organization cuts when the going gets tough, but, dollar for dollar, they are among the most cost-effective forms of compensation that you can offer.

Come to think of it, this list of tips for enchanting volunteers is equally applicable to your employees. So now that you know how to enchant your employees and volunteers, go forth and flourish.

My Personal Story, by Milene Laube Dutra

Milene Laube Dutra is a marketing and communications consultant based in São Paulo, Brazil. In this personal story, she explains how a toothpaste company she worked for enchanted her with a machine. (I'm not making this up.)

I AM NOT GOING TO TALK ABOUT MY KIDS BECAUSE I BELIEVE THIS IS the very special moment in everyone's life. Instead, I am going to share my first day as a trainee in an oral care company (formerly Anakol do Brasil, subsequently acquired by Colgate-Palmolive).

How can someone be enchanted by a dental-cream company? I was twenty years old, still a marketing student at ESPM (Escola Superior de Propaganda e Marketing), and had landed in my first marketing dream job as marketing trainee/intern.

One day it was Plant Day, and we were going to see the production site! I had never, ever been to a plant and never saw how products were made. I saw them on the shelves and that was it! My heart started pounding when I saw that huge toothpaste tube maker. It was as tall as a tree and as wide as a truck. I felt like small David in front of Goliath.

In one side of this machine tiny aluminum coins were dropped in a big funnel. Noise, smoke and heat . . . the coins started traveling through the machine. They stopped, and there was a punch. The coins magically transformed into tubes! Then the tubes go through the printing process and become alive with the product's brand/logo. At the end of the process, fully printed toothpaste tubes with caps were gathered in carton boxes to be carried to the next step: the filling line.

I started thinking about all the things that were produced, and all the different plants that intelligent engineers had built. That day I became a product manager, and since then my passion for new products/innovation—especially consumer goods that are made in plants—grew as I developed many new products for different industries and visited several different plants in Brazil and abroad.

Chapter 11

How to Enchant Your Boss

By working faithfully eight hours a day, you may eventually
get to be a boss and work twelve hours a day.

—Robert Frost

Whether you like your boss or not, she controls what you get out of your job. I'm not referring only to money—there's also satisfaction, advancement, visibility, and perks. This chapter explains how to enchant your boss. I start with a humdinger of a recommendation about prioritization, so get ready.

Make Your Boss Look Good

It's humdinger time. The best way to enchant your boss is to make her look good. That's right: Make your boss look good. Sure, changing the world, delighting customers, and increasing shareholder value are all part of the big picture, but making your boss look good is your day-to-day job.

You should do this within the boundaries of ethics and morality, but the reality is that when your boss looks good, you look good. When your boss advances, you advance. And when your boss implodes, you implode.

Forget any fantasies of outshining your boss and replacing or rising above her. I've never seen a case where a boss's boss says, "We need to promote that person above her manager."

It takes most people years to understand the wisdom of making your boss look good—often by learning it the hard way. If you can internalize and implement this concept, you're 90 percent of the way to enchanting your boss.

Drop Everything and Do What Your Boss Asks

> Priority is a function of context.
>
> —Stephen Covey

Suppose your boss asks you to do some research about your competition. You know she could do it herself, and you think she won't use the results anyway. Meanwhile, you are up to your eyeballs in work because you are writing a manual that is critical for shipping.

Do you (a) finish the manual or (b) drop everything and do what she asked?

You may pride yourself on your ability to prioritize what's most important for the big picture. You may think you should explain why the manual is more important than the research. You may think you'd be remiss to not finish the manual first. Let me break this to you gently: Drop everything and do what your boss asked you to do if you want to enchant her.

It doesn't matter how suboptimal this might be. For all you know, your boss's boss asked for the research, so what you may consider a poor use of time is important to your boss (especially if your boss has read this book and is trying to enchant *her* boss). No matter what the reason—and even if there is no good reason—do what your boss asked first. The goal is to convince your boss that you are hardworking, efficient, and effective—not that you know how to establish priorities.

By the way, this is also a good strategy for husbands. If your wife asks you to do something, drop everything and do it. You may not think it's important, but you aren't juggling four kids, a career, and several charitable causes. You may think you see the "big picture," but you don't see *her* big picture. This advice alone justifies buying *Enchantment*.

Underpromise, Overdeliver

Assuming you haven't stopped reading or puked because of my recommendation to drop everything for your boss, the next step is to underpromise and overdeliver. To understand this concept, you can think of your boss in two ways: first, as your most important reference account. You never want to underdeliver to such an important customer.

Second, as a guest at Disneyland. Did you know that signs telling you how long you'll have to wait to get on rides at Disneyland are overstated? Then, when you get to the front of the line in less time than you expected, you're a happy vacationer.

If you're wondering if I'm advising you to sandbag your boss, the answer is that I am. Specifically, whenever you can, set a goal that you're 120 percent sure you can hit in 80 percent of the allotted time.

People who underpromise and overdeliver are more enchanting. Coming close and making a great effort is only good for kids, inspirational movies, horseshoes, and hand grenades. In other circumstances, you either deliver or you don't.

Prototype Your Work

In a blog post called "3 Things to Make Your Manager Worship You," Scot Herrick explains the enchanting power of prototyping your work.* When you get an assignment from your boss, you should quickly complete part of the task and ask for feedback.

---

* Scot Herrick, "3 Things to Make Your Manager Worship You," Cube Rules (blog), August 20, 2009, http://cuberules.com/2009/08/20/3-things-to-make-your-manager-worship-you.

This gives your boss the opportunity to make course corrections early in the process—increasing the probability you'll deliver what she wanted. Plus, your boss will think you are "proactive" instead of a "doesn't get things right" employee.

Discussing options is also useful at this early stage. Your prototype is heading in one direction, but other directions are also viable and perhaps better. The act of prototyping is often a catalyst that makes people think of other possibilities.

So, the next time your boss asks you to prepare a report or a PowerPoint presentation, work up a quick outline in a few hours, and show her what you're thinking, to catalyze a discussion of options. This is bound to enchant her and produce better results.

Show and Broadcast Progress

After the prototype stage, you should demonstrate that you're making progress on projects that take weeks or months to complete. Don't be a pain in the ass by micro-communicating each small step, but ensuring that she never has to ask how things are going keeps you and the project on her radar.

Showing progress isn't for your boss's eyes only—it's for anyone who needs to know. "Broadcast" is too strong a word, but hiding your accomplishments under a bushel isn't the right practice, either. If you don't toot your own horn, don't complain that there's no music.

You should show progress without antagonizing other people in the organization. Here's how to make this happen in an enchanting way:

- Provide the facts with no embellishment and exaggeration—in other words, underbroadcast and overdeliver.
- Credit everyone who helped make the success happen. Be generous in praise and spreading out the glory.
- Let other people announce the good news for you if possible—for example, a customer calling your boss or, even better, your boss's boss.

- Make your wins your boss's wins, too. The more wins you cause your boss to bask in, the more enchanting you are.

You may not enjoy broadcasting your wins, but it is part of good personal branding and a means to enchant your boss. Give it a try— I'm sure you'll get used to it, but don't get addicted to it, because then you'll stop being enchanting.

Form Friendships

Employees with many professional friendships are more enchanting, because these relationships make them more effective employees and provide social proof of their wonderfulness. Here's how this works:

- **Forming friendships makes you more efficient and effective.** It's easier to do business with friends. They are more likely to help you— and you are more likely to reciprocate. Acting friendly also takes less energy than acting angry and antagonistic.
- **Friends beget more friends.** Making friends is an upward spiral: the more friends you have, the more friends you make, because people take their cues from others. The more friends you make, the more efficient and effective you are. And the more efficient and effective you are, the more you will enchant your boss.
- **Many friends create a halo.** The math is simple: If a friend of a friend is your friend, then the more friends you have, the more friends of friends you have. This halo transfers to your boss, too, so if you're popular and enchanting, people will assume your boss is popular and enchanting, too. At least they will give her the benefit of the doubt.
- **People don't screw around with people with many friends.** If others view you as a good, popular, and enchanting person, you create your own base of power. Then, let me be honest, your boss will hesitate to screw with you. There is nothing wrong with a person who is enchanting and powerful at the same time.

Only positive results accrue for people who are popular in the workplace, and this benefits both you and your boss.

Ask for Mentoring

In chapter 2: "How to Achieve Likability," I wrote that everybody is good at something. This even includes your boss; she's bound to possess some knowledge that is useful to you. Asking for her mentoring is a twofer: You get the benefit of her help, plus you flatter her by asking.

Only a sociopath would not be flattered, and if you work for a sociopath, you should focus on getting away from him, not enchanting him, anyway. If your boss agrees, you must heed the advice, because not listening can backfire on you. If your boss doesn't agree, you still reap the benefits of flattering her for asking.

I've had two great mentors in my career. First, Marty Gruber of Nova Stylings was my boss in the jewelry manufacturing business, and he taught me the most important lesson of all: how to sell. The jewelry business is a tough one because the raw materials—gold and diamonds—are commodities that any store buyer can price. Any margin over the base cost of gold and diamonds value is "enchantment."

Second, Al Eisenstat was the general counsel and godfather of Apple when I worked there. He helped me escape unscathed from the epic internal battles between various Apple fiefdumbs [sic]. He taught me how to survive in a highly political environment—to the extent that I could learn this skill, anyway.

Deliver Bad News Early

There are two kind of news that you can bring to your boss: good news and bad news. Good news is no problem—everyone loves good news.

Bad news is the challenge—for example, a schedule slipped, a sale fell through, or users discovered a bug in your software. Scot Herrick, the author of "3 Things to Make Your Manager Worship You," recommends delivering bad news as soon as possible, because good bosses want bad news early so that there are more opportunities to fix the problem.

Bad bosses only want good news, however, because they prefer to live in a bubble. The problem is, when the bubble pops, you'll go down with the bad boss. Do what you can to avoid working for people who only want good news.

Two more pieces of advice about bad news: First, don't blame anyone—especially your boss—for what happened. You may even want to take the blame. Second, don't just tell your boss the bad news. Show up with ideas to fix the problem, too. You'll look proactive and on top of things—which will surely enchant your boss.

My Personal Story, by David Stockwell

Dave Stockwell is a founding partner of Seasonal View, a customer-service consultancy firm, in Tacoma, Washington. In this personal story, he describes an employee who totally enchanted him while he was working at REI.

MY ENCHANTMENT CAME A HANDFUL OF YEARS AGO BY WAY OF AN intern named Angelica Gonzales. I was managing the help desk at REI and had agreed to take on a handful of students from the King County Digital Bridge program. This program takes students who have failed in the traditional school system and teaches them tech skills while they work toward their GED. The students who perform at the top of their class are rewarded with an internship at a local company to learn what it's like working in corporate life.

Angelica was unique. Born into a homeless family, she survived gang life, and at age sixteen she got pregnant. When she began at REI, she immediately took to learning as much about working in a corporation as possible. I answered questions every day, as she never ceased to explore not only the technical side of supporting an organization but also how the people worked together.

As the world of technical support is a constant firefight, her ability to ecstatically go about the most mundane tasks as she continued to learn about herself and the world around her created an aura of positive energy that spilled over to the rest of the team. When her internship wrapped up, I hired her as a junior technician to put her newfound tech skills to use.

She once popped into my office to ask a question. After I answered her, she paused and then asked, "Can someone like me ever be a CEO?" That's when I fully realized the difference in support and mentoring that I had received in my life versus what she had when she was growing up.

Since that day I've taken the energy and, for lack of a better phrase, "sparkle of magic" with me in my interactions with my employees, peers, boss, and especially my customers. Realizing that people's desire can be so strong, if they can find a goal that they wish to achieve, has helped me to improve my interaction with people.

Chapter 12

How to Resist Enchantment

For a successful technology, reality must take precedence over public relations, for nature cannot be fooled.

—Richard Feynman

Many people have embraced the techniques of enchantment, influence, and persuasion. Unfortunately, they are not all good folks with great causes who have your best interests at heart. For this reason, I'm including a chapter that explains how to resist their kind of enchantment. And here's a bonus: If you understand how to resist enchantment, you will be a better enchanter.

Avoid Tempting Situations

Not everyone is an ethical enchanter, and even ethical enchanters can convince you to do something that's not in your best interest. Plus, there's the "third-person effect"—the observation that people exposed to mass-media persuasion believe that others are more affected by it than they are. In other words, you could be in over your head.

Avoiding tempting situations (store sales), events (auctions), locations (outlet malls), and times (shopping with girlfriends) is the simplest technique to resist enchantment. If you're not exposed to temptation, you're less likely to make a bad decision.

You can also delay making decisions if avoidance isn't possible. For example, if an item on sale is tempting you, tell yourself that you'll come back at the end of your shopping trip to get it. Delaying is most important when you're stressed, tired, or sick, because that's when you're apt to make a decision you'll regret.

If someone presses you for a quick decision, remember the phrase "Dopeler effect." It appeared as an entry in the 1998 *Washington Post* contest for inventing new words, and it's perfect for this situation: "Dopeler effect (n): The tendency of stupid ideas to seem smarter when they come at you rapidly."

So step one in resisting enchantment is simple: Avoid situations that may tempt you into doing something that isn't in your best interest.

Look Far into the Future

If you can't avoid tempting situations, then at least ask this question: What will the impact of this decision be a year from now? People make poor decisions because they think about the past ("I should have . . .") and the near future ("It sure would be fun to . . ."), but not the future.

Consider the impact your current actions will make in a year or more. A negative or even neutral outcome wastes your time and resources and leads to disenchantment. If the far-future benefits look good, then allow the enchantment to take place.

The issue is not as simple as, "I need to think about expensive items, but I can go for cheap ones." As a wise grandmother of Sasha Aickin, vice president of engineering of an online real-estate firm called Redfin, once advised, "When you buy something cheap and bad, the best you're going to feel about it is when you buy it. When you buy something expensive and good, the worst you're going to feel about it is when you buy it."*

Know Your Limitations

Do you wonder why rich, famous, and seemingly intelligent people get swindled? It's because they don't know what they don't know, and they won't admit that they don't know everything.

There is an additional kind of limitation: outright limits to the scope of human knowledge. No one may know how something works, and no one can predict the future. This is good to remember when you experience delusions of omniscience.

Getting to know your limitations is difficult—so difficult that you might want to seek outside help. Remember how the devil's advocate of the Catholic Church found faults in candidates for sainthood? You could find a devil's advocate to find fault in the propositions and temptations that you face.

This person's role is to find holes in your logic, take the long view, see the big picture, and prevent you from making mistakes. She is also a useful disengagement tool: "My devil's advocate doesn't think I should do this" is a reasonable way to say no.

If nothing else, becoming aware of your limitations, the limitations of knowledge in general, and the outside perspective of a personal devil's advocate will lead you to make sound, informed decisions.

Beware of Pseudo Salience, Data, and Experts

> What luck for rulers that men do not think.
>
> **—Adolf Hitler**

Salient points are good things. For example, the number of songs a music player can hold versus its capacity in gigabytes is useful. Pseudo

---

* Glen Kelman, "Groupon's Success Disaster," Redfin Corporate Blog, September 16, 2010, http://blog.redfin.com/blog/2010/09/groupons_success_disaster.html.

salience, however, is deceptive. If a phone carrier says its phone is free, you might think that's a great deal, until you discover that it requires a two-year subscription with a large early-termination penalty.

Data are good, but correlation doesn't equal causation. For example, Harvard researchers measured the vocal pitch of forty-nine men from a tribe in Tanzania and compared that to the number of children they fathered.* They found that the deeper the man's voice, the more children he had.

Does this mean that the deeper a man's voice, the more fertile he is? Not necessarily. Maybe men with many children have lower voices because they have to yell all the time. Their children caused the lower voices, not vice versa.

According to Michael Mauboussin, author of *Think Twice: Harnessing the Power of Counterintuition,* three conditions must exist for X to cause Y: first, X must happen before Y; second, X and Y must have a functional relationship, not a coincidental one; and third, there cannot be another factor, call it Z, that causes both X and Y.†

Did the Tanzanian men with more children have lower voices before they became fathers? Is there a functional relationship between lower voices and more children? Could anything else have caused these men to have more children and lower voices?

Experts are helpful except when they're wrong. The problem is, people tend to believe experts even if they *are* wrong. You should exercise the most caution when expert advice is groundbreaking, is too good to be true, attracts a great deal of popular attention, comes from a source with impressive credentials in an impressive journal, or receives the support of an entity that stands to gain from people believing the advice.‡

---

* David H. Freedman, *Wrong: Why Experts Keep Failing Us—and How to Know When Not to Trust Them* (New York: Little, Brown, 2010), 42.

† Michael J. Mauboussin, *Think Twice: Harnessing the Power of Counterintuition* (Boston: Harvard Business Press, 2009), 95.

‡ David H. Freedman, *Wrong: Why Experts Keep Failing Us—and How to Know When Not to Trust Them* (New York: Little, Brown, 2010), 217–24.

Don't Fall for the Example of One

The plural of "anecdote" is not data.

—Ben Goldacre

In chapter 4, "How to Prepare," I explained the power of using one evocative example. You should assume other people have figured out how to use such powerful examples, too. A great picture, concrete imagery (thousands of pairs of shoes), or a personal story doesn't necessarily mean a cause is true, good, important, or relevant, however.

For example, measles is making a comeback in the United States, because parents are not vaccinating their children. Despite the scientific evidence to the contrary, they believe the MMR (measles, mumps, rubella) vaccination causes autism. Jenny McCarthy, a model, actress, and mother of an autistic child, is a highly visible spokesperson for Generation Rescue, a research organization for the causes and cures for autism. Her visibility on television shows exposed her beliefs to millions of people.

McCarthy also received exposure from the James Randi Educational Foundation when she won its Pigasus Award in 2008. The foundation gave this award to her as the "performer who fooled the greatest number of people with the least effort." So here is McCarthy, with a sample group of one, plus stories she's heard, telling parents one thing while volumes of medical and scientific research are indicating to parents something completely different.

While there is a chance that she and others who believe MMR causes autism are right, the preponderance of research says they are wrong. In this kind of situation, one glaring data point doesn't determine a trend, so don't let it sway you.

Defy the Crowd

Skepticism is the beginning of Faith.   **—Oscar Wilde**

The power of social acceptance should make you skeptical (though not necessarily cynical) about the wisdom of the crowd. Sometimes the outcome of a decision isn't important enough to sweat the validity of the crowd—for example, picking a movie, even though it's not sold out.

But for bigger decisions, it's good to remember that the wisdom of the crowd is often less than it's cracked up to be. The classic example is tulip mania, during which, in the 1630s, an irrational desire for the flower encouraged people in the Netherlands to drive up the price of tulips. We (that is, Silicon Valley) were no smarter in the dot-com days of the 1990s, when we drove the stock prices of Internet companies to insane levels.

Crowd mentality doesn't affect only the great unwashed masses. Physicist Richard Feynman served on the Rogers Commission, which investigated the crash of the Challenger space shuttle. The Commission was hardly a group of flunkies, because it included people such as Chuck Yeager, Neil Armstrong, and Sally Ride.

This text comes from the conclusion of Feynman's personal observations about the cause of the crash:

> If a reasonable launch schedule is to be maintained, engineering often cannot be done fast enough to keep up with the expectations of originally conservative certification criteria designed to guarantee a very safe vehicle. In these situations, subtly, and often with apparently logical arguments, the criteria are altered so that flights may still be certified in time. They therefore fly in a relatively unsafe condition, with a chance of failure of the order of a percent (it is difficult to be more accurate).

> Official management, on the other hand, claims to believe the

probability of failure is a thousand times less. One reason for this may be an attempt to assure the government of NASA perfection and success in order to ensure the supply of funds. The other may be that they sincerely believed it to be true, demonstrating an almost incredible lack of communication between themselves and their working engineers.*

Feynman threatened to withdraw his name from the report if the commission did not publish his personal observations. He also used a key persuasion technique by telling a story of how he immersed an O-ring, the defective part that caused the crash, in ice water, and it lost resiliency.

According to Michael J. Mauboussin, author of *Think Twice*, three conditions are necessary for the crowd to communicate genuine wisdom: first, diversity in the members of the crowd; second, consideration of everyone's opinion in the crowd; and third, incentives that encourage only people with insights to participate.† If you're thinking of going with the crowd, ensure that these conditions are present.

Track Previous Decisions

When making a decision, ask yourself, "What happened when I did something like this before?" If the answer is something bad or less than optimal, then this question should jar you into not repeating a mistake. This doesn't mean you should not try something again, but at least you should reap the benefit of knowledge gained from past failures.

---

* Richard Feynman, *Report of the Presidential Commission on the Space Shuttle Challenger Accident,* volume 2, appendix F, "Personal Observations on Reliability of Shuttle," May 27, 1986, http://history.nasa.gov/rogersrep/v2appf.htm.
† Michael J. Mauboussin, *Think Twice: Harnessing the Power of Counterintuition* (Boston: Harvard Business Press, 2009), 47.

A written journal of your decision making is a useful tool to track your history. If you do fail at something, you might as well learn from it in a postmortem. Scott Berkun, author of *Confessions of a Public Speaker,* provides this definitive list of questions to ask to track previous decisions:

- What was the probable sequence of events?
- Were there multiple small mistakes which led to a larger one?
- Were there any erroneous assumptions made?
- Did we have the right goals? Were we trying to solve the right problem?
- Was it possible to have recognized bad assumptions earlier?
- What do we know now that would have been useful then?
- What would we do differently in that exact situation if we were to relive it?
- Was this mistake impossible to avoid?
- Has enough time passed for us to know if this is a mistake or not?*

It's one thing to be enchanted the first time and experience a negative outcome. It's another to let this happen repeatedly, so track your decisions and look for patterns of behavior.

Let Yourself Be Enchanted in Small Ways

An alternative to the hard-ass practices we've just discussed is to allow people to enchant you but only in small ways. Then you can save your energy for the big battles and not think of yourself as a constant naysayer.

Is there any harm if a waiter persuades you to order dessert?

---

* Scott Berkun, "How to Learn from Your Mistakes," Scott Berkun (blog), July 17, 2005, www.scottberkun.com/essays/44-how-to-learn-from-your-mistakes.

Is there any harm if your daughter enchants you into buying her another Webkinz? Is there any harm if you skip a lunch meeting to play hockey? By giving in to small enchantments, you can save your resistance for the decisions that can affect your life in serious ways.

You may even find such joy in small enchantments that it reduces the seeming importance of the big, risky, and expensive ones. We may have a limited capacity to resist, so we should save our capacity for the major decisions.

Create a Checklist

Finally, let's return to our friend the checklist. When faced with an enchanting proposition, it's useful to go through a checklist of the critical factors to consider. Here's a starting point for you:

- If I waited a week, I'd still make the same decision.
- A year from now, this decision will still be a good one.
- I've done my homework by reading independent reports and reviews of the product/service/organization/idea.
- I am fully aware of the total cost of this decision, including installation, support, maintenance, subscriptions, and upgrades.
- This decision will not harm people.
- This decision will not unduly harm the environment.
- This decision isn't unethical, immoral, or illegal.
- This decision will not set a bad example for my children.
- If no one could see that I was doing this, I would still do it.
- If everyone could see that I was doing this, I would still do it.

Honestly, looking back, I would have made dozens of decisions differently if I had consulted a checklist like this one. As the saying goes, "Better late than never!"

My Personal Story, by Tibor Kruska

Tibor Kruska is an information technology entrepreneur from Dorog, Hungary. I included his personal story at the end of the chapter about resisting enchantment to show you that if something is good enough, resistance is futile. :-)

THIS IS NOT A FAKE STORY JUST TO MAKE YOU HAPPY. THIS IS MY real story of enchantment with your book. I like reading business books; I have a lot, about three hundred. Most of them are pretty good, but if I should give away all but one, I would keep *The Art of the Start*.

Years back, a friend of mine sent me a video about your presentation of this book at TiECon, 2006. I am not kidding: I watched it hundreds of times (just check out my iPod), before I could buy the book.

I even went to the US from Europe to buy this book! (OK, this is not quite true, because I went to a conference in Las Vegas, anyway, but I bought your book on the same trip.)

Comparing most business books to yours, almost everything is just crap—at least when you expect real, practical advice for entrepreneurs. I simply wouldn't let anyone start a new business before reading *The Art of the Start*.

I hate the books about subjects like think-hard-you're-smart, repeat-every-morning-I'm-positive, or even you-can-do-it-just-set-your-mind-to-it. If I need to set my mind, I'm practically mindless! Hence, it is the worst start to be an entrepreneur.

Your book doesn't tell me what should I think or force myself to think, but it DOES tell me what to DO. This is exactly what I need when launching a new business. In fact, I read it before EVERY new project I start.

Conclusion

Into the sunset's turquoise marge
The moon dips, like a pearly barge
Enchantment sails through magic seas,
To faeryland Hesperides,
Over the hills and away.

—Madison Julius Cawein

I hope reading *Enchantment* was a worthwhile and enjoyable experience. I leave you with all that I know about the art of enchantment. Now your task is to apply this knowledge, reject what doesn't work, and enhance what does. Ever clever, we designed the table of contents as a checklist to help you measure your progress. If you want to measure your knowledge of enchantment, take Guy's Realistic Enchantment Aptitude Test (GREAT) at the end of this section.

One last thought: Enchantment is a powerful skill, and with power comes responsibility. It's your duty to use these skills in a manner that benefits all the parties involved, if not the world. Please keep this thought in mind as you go forth.

Be well, do good, and kick butt,

Guy Kawasaki

My Personal Story, by Kathy Parsanko

Kathy Parsanko, a marketing and PR consultant in Cincinnati, Ohio, was working for the Drake Center when she shared this final personal story of the book. What's the ultimate form of enchantment? The long-term love between two people.

DON MARTIN AND ULYS MARTIN, WHOM DON CALLS HIS "LOVELY bride," live at Bridgeway Pointe, the Drake Center's assisted-living community. Don lives in an apartment on his own. Ulys lives in the secured dementia unit on a separate floor. He rides his electric wheelchair to visit her day and night. They have been married for sixty-five years, lived throughout the world, and now they're here.

She shuffles and often doesn't know what day it is, where she is, and may not know whom she is talking to . . . until Don appears. Whenever she sees him, she completely lights up, smiles, and sometimes I see tears. She knows Don, all right. And they communicate—with and without words. This is the kind of love many think exists only in novels and dreams. But I've witnessed it.

Ulys and Don's story was on the front page of the *Cincinnati Enquirer* Valentine's Day weekend in 2010. At first, Don didn't understand why anyone would want to read a story about "us." He didn't understand what all the fuss was about. But then he got it. I read him all the positive, glowing comments that readers wrote online. Many thanked the couple for giving them hope that they, too, would find true love someday.

Working in PR/community relations for an assisted-living community has been life affirming. By the time they come to assisted living, residents and their families are often vulnerable and stripped of all pretenses. The majority of these folks know "what truly matters," and that's love. And there's nothing more enchanting than being in the midst of it.

GREAT Test

To get you started, I answered the first two questions for you.

1. How many muscles are used to make an enchanting smile?

   a. <u>0</u>
   b. 2
   c. 3
   d. 5
   e. 10

2. How should you dress compared to the people you want to enchant?

   a. Better than them
   b. Worse than them
   c. <u>Equal to them</u>
   d. It doesn't matter
   e. To please yourself

3. Which methods are useful to launch a cause?

   a. Tell a story
   b. Plant many seeds
   c. Ask people what they're going to do
   d. Reduce the number of choices
   e. All of the above

4. When you meet a person for the first time, you should

   a. Consider his requests with skepticism
   b. Shake his hand for at least ten seconds
   c. Use war analogies to break the ice
   d. Avoid idle chat about personal passions and focus on work-related subjects
   e. Default to a yes attitude and determine how you can help him

5. **The five qualities of a great cause are:**

   a. Dumb, insufficient, clueless, exasperating, and expensive

   b. Deep, intelligent, complete, empowering, and elegant

   c. Detrimental, inept, conflicted, erotic, and ephemeral

   d. Deep, intellectual, competitive, eloquent, and exotic

   e. Didactic, insipid, cunning, earnest, and ecclesiastical

6. **Select the third quality of good messaging: short, sweet, and**

   a. Serious

   b. Suave

   c. Cynical

   d. Swallowable

   e. Sanctimonious

7. **Which characteristics encourage someone to try out your product?**

   a. Ease of use

   b. Immediacy of starting

   c. Low cost of trial

   d. Reversibility of trial

   e. All of the above

8. **When should you disclose any conflicts of interest?**

   a. Immediately after closing the deal

   b. Never

   c. At the very start of a relationship

   d. When asked by the other party

   e. When you've been subpoenaed

9. **Which method cannot help overcome resistance to a cause?**

   a. Creating the perception of ubiquity

   b. Creating the perception of scarcity

   c. Finding a bright spot

   d. Showing people your magic

   e. All the methods can help overcome resistance

10. **When people thank you for a favor, the optimal response is**

   a. "You're welcome"
   b. "You owe me now"
   c. "It was nothing"
   d. "My people did it anyway"
   e. "I know you'd do the same for me"

11. **Which is the false statement?**

   a. You should create a separate workspace for believers
   b. People will reciprocate good deeds many decades later
   c. A homogeneous team makes enchantment endure
   d. The Grateful Dead allows people to tape their concerts
   e. Financial rewards may not ensure loyalty and support

12. **What is the ideal format of a PowerPoint or Keynote presentation?**

   a. Sixty slides, sixty minutes, six point font
   b. Ten slides, sixty minutes, eight point font
   c. Twenty slides, twenty minutes, ten point font
   d. Ten slides, twenty minutes, thirty point font
   e. Thirty slides, ninety minutes, sixty point font

13. **What is the ideal length of an enchanting YouTube video?**

   a. Sixty minutes
   b. Sixty seconds
   c. Five minutes
   d. Fifteen minutes
   e. Ten seconds

14. **Which Japanese concept should you not practice?**

   a. *Wa*
   b. *Bakatare*
   c. *Shibui*
   d. *Seijaku*
   e. *Kanso*

15. When should you heed the crowd?

    a. The crowd represents diverse backgrounds

    b. Everyone's opinion in the crowd is considered

    c. There are incentives that encourage only people with insights to participate

    d. a, b, and c

    e. c only

16. What can you do to virtually guarantee enchanting an audience at the beginning of a speech?

    a. Thank the audience for turning off their cell phones

    b. Offer a discount for your product or service

    c. Show pictures of what enchants you about their city

    d. Show pictures of your new Porsche

    e. Explain that you're exhausted after a long plane ride

17. What should you not do if you want to enchant your employees?

    a. Enable them to work independently

    b. Ask them to do what you wouldn't do

    c. Address your own shortcomings first

    d. Celebrate team successes

    e. Judge your results and their intentions

18. If you ever want me to stay in your hotel, what should you not do?

    a. Charge for WiFi access

    b. Provide only one electrical outlet near the desk

    c. Convert the fitness center into more guest rooms

    d. Charge a fee to make a reservation

    e. Provide only one honor-bar key

19. What is the most important thing you can do to enchant your boss?

    a. Suck up

    b. Deliver bad news at the last possible moment

c. Refuse career advice

d. Underpromise and overdeliver

e. Drop everything and do what your boss asks first

20. What is not a quality of Twitter?

a. Reliable

b. Free

c. Easy

d. Ubiquitous

e. Fast

Extra credit: I answered the first two questions of this test in order to

a. Increase scores

b. Show you that I know my material

c. Shorten the length of the test

d. Encourage cheating

e. Encourage you to take the test

Answers: 1 b, 2 c, 3 e, 4 e, 5 b, 6 d, 7 e, 8 c, 9 e, 10 e, 11 c, 12 d, 13 b, 14 b, 15 d, 16 c, 17 b, 18 d, 19 e, 20 a

How did you do? Here's a rough guideline to measure your enchantment skills:

19–20 You could teach Steve Jobs a thing or two

16–18 Go forth and enchant

11–15 Read *Enchantment* one more time

6–10 Consider a job involving little human contact

0–5 Ask me for a refund

Selected Bibliography

That is a good book which is opened with expectation,
and closed with delight and profit.

—A. Bronson Alcott

Over the course of the year that I spent writing this book, I consulted approximately twenty books about influence and persuasion. They expanded and enriched my concept of enchantment. I list them here so you can trace my footsteps and dig deeper into the methods of enchantment.

Bedell, Gene. *3 Steps to Yes: The Gentle Art of Getting Your Way.* New York: Crown Business, 2000.

Brafman, Ori, and Rom Brafman. *Sway: The Irresistible Pull of Irrational Behavior.* New York: Broadway Business, 2008.

Brafman, Ori, and Rom Brafman. *Click: The Magic of Instant Connections.* New York: Broadway Business, 2010.

Carnegie, Dale. *How to Win Friends and Influence People.* New York: Simon and Schuster, 2009.

Cialdini, Robert. *Influence: The Psychology of Persuasion.* New York: Harper Paperbacks, 2006.

Deci, Edward L., with Richard Flaste. *Why We Do What We Do: Understanding Self-Motivation*. New York: Putnam's, 1995.

Earls, Mark. *Herd: How to Change Mass Behavior by Harnessing Our True Nature*. West Sussex, UK: John Wiley, 2007.

Fisher, Len. *The Perfect Swarm: The Science of Complexity in Everyday Life*. New York: Basic Books, 2009.

Freedman, David H. *Wrong: Why Experts Keep Failing Us—and How to Know When Not to Trust Them*. New York: Little, Brown, 2010.

Gawande, Atul. *The Checklist Manifesto: How to Get Things Right*. New York: Metropolitan Books, 2010.

Goldstein, Noah J., Steve J. Martin, and Robert B. Cialdini. *Yes! 50 Scientifically Proven Ways to be Persuasive*. New York: Free Press, 2008.

Granger, Russell H. *The 7 Triggers to Yes: The New Science Behind Influencing People's Decisions*. New York: McGraw-Hill, 2008.

Heath, Chip, and Dan Heath. *Switch: How to Change Things When Change Is Hard*. New York: Broadway Books, 2010.

Lehrer, Jonah. *How We Decide*. Boston: Houghton Mifflin Harcourt, 2009.

Lovaglia, Michael J. *Knowing People: The Personal Use of Social Psychology*. New York: McGraw-Hill, 1999.

Luntz, Frank. *Words That Work: It's Not What You Say, It's What People Hear*. New York: Hyperion, 2007.

Mauboussin, Michael J. *Think Twice: Harnessing the Power of Counterintuition*. Boston: Harvard Business Press, 2009.

Patterson, Kerry, Joseph Grenny, David Maxfield, Ron McMillan, and Al Switzler. *Influencer: The Power to Change Anything*. New York: McGraw-Hill, 2008.

Shell, G. Richard, and Mario Moussa. *The Art of Woo: Using Strategic Persuasion to Sell Your Ideas*. New York: Portfolio, 2007.

Thaler, Richard H., and Cass R. Sunstein. *Nudge: Improving Decisions About Health, Wealth, and Happiness*. New York: Penguin Books, 2009.

Index

Because he did not have time to read every new book in his field, the great Polish anthropologist Bronislaw Malinowski used a simple and efficient method of deciding which ones were worth his attention: Upon receiving a new book, he immediately checked the index to see if his name was cited, and how often. The more "Malinowski" the more compelling the book. No "Malinowski," and he doubted the subject of the book was anthropology at all.

—Neil Postman

I hope Robert Cialdini checks this index.

—Guy Kawasaki

Coverphon

I love to hear a choir. I love the humanity to see the faces
of real people devoting themselves to a piece of music.
I like the teamwork. It makes me feel optimistic about the
human race when I see them cooperating like that.

—Paul McCartney

Under the Cover: How It Took 260 People to Make This Cover

The cover of *Enchantment* has its own enchanting story. Illustrating the concept of enchantment is difficult, and I wanted to see what it meant to many people and how they would graphically represent it. The straightest path to this goal was a design contest. My theory is, the more great minds working on a task, the better the results. I contacted my buddies at CrowdSpring, and we created a contest with a $1,000 prize. To my amazement, approximately 250 people entered 760 designs. This is roughly seventy-five times more designs than most authors see. I narrowed down the 760 entries to these five and enabled people to vote for their favorite.

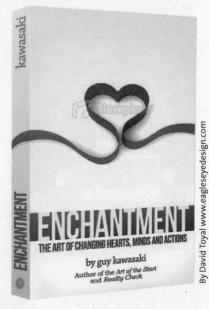

By Richard Klasovsky

By David Toyal www.eagleseyedesign.com

The entry that received the most votes was the one with the blue butterfly on the red cover. The designer of this cover used this stock photo by Enchantedgal (I'm not making this up) on DeviantART.

By Kimberly Crick www.TheEnchantedGallery.com

I liked this design the most, too. I was prepared to override the popular vote, but the tally meant that I could maintain the illusion of impartiality, openness, and transparency. :-) So much the better.

During the contest, many designers attacked me for the heinous exploitation of their colleagues' creativity. Their math was that 250 people entered and only one won, so I exploited the other 249. The crime is called *spec work* because it's speculative and without a guarantee of compensation. Hello? Life is spec work: no guts, no glory, no visibility, no experience, and no prize. I didn't force anyone to enter, and this was a chance to make $1,000 and gain visibility. Much to my delight, the winner was (a) not a "professional" designer; (b) not an American; and (c) not an orifice. He was Ade Harnusa Azril, an electrical engineering undergraduate student at the Institut Teknologi Bandung in Indonesia.

I could not have planned it better.

After I announced the winner, designers attacked the winning entry as nothing more than a "stock photo of a butterfly on a red background." Yup, and Andy Warhol painted a Campbell soup can.

Too bad they didn't think of that too, huh? I don't know any industry where people get their rocks off by tearing each other apart as much as graphic design.

Unfortunately (or perhaps fortunately as you will learn), the design didn't go over well with the editor, publicist, publisher, and assistant publisher. "Too New Age." "Too feminine—no man would be caught reading a red book with a butterfly on the cover." "Too self-help, too touchy-feely, too . . ." you get the picture. And the most damning of all was, "The sales force hates it."

Welcome to my life.

But 90 percent of the battle is showing up. The other 90 percent is persevering after you show up.

With hindsight this negative reaction forced me outside the comfort zone. One night, while pedaling a Star Trac recumbent bike while reading tweets on my iPad watching *NHL On the Fly*, I came up with the idea of an origami butterfly. This took care of two issues: no more "stock photo" stigma and fewer self-help, New-Age connotations. Plus, there was a great tie-in: Japanese guy and Japanese art form.

I didn't know a thing about origami, however, so I searched for "origami butterfly" on Google, and I asked my 330,000 closest friends on Twitter, "Anyone know an origami master?" This yielded great results. My sister—Jean Okimoto—as well as Lisa "Kailua Lisa" Mullinaux, Jason Wehmhoener, and Marco Carbullido came to my assistance, too. These efforts led me to Michael G. LaFosse and a design called the "Alexander Swallowtail butterfly," which I saw at Sara Adams's Web site:

Come to find out, Michael is the Wayne Gretzky of origami. He and his partner, Richard Alexander, run Origamido Studio. Michael was featured in the great origami movie, *Between the Folds*. I went to the Origamido Web site and sent an e-mail to the address that usually goes to webmasters who never respond. Lo and behold, Michael answered in a day.

One thing led to another—including tales of the International Marketplace in Waikiki and Don Ho—and Michael created a custom design called the "Kawasaki Swallowtail." Ever heard of a Jobs, Gates, Williams, Stone, Ballmer, Ellison, or Zuckerberg origami butterfly? I didn't think so.

Richard pasted gold paper that he handmade to a printed sheet of washi to create the double-sided effect. Then Michael folded the Kawasaki Swallowtail, and voila, I had a badass custom butterfly that looks like James Clavell's *Shogun* meets B-1 stealth bomber.

At that point I had the badass butterfly and the concept of a badass butterfly on a red gradient. Now I needed someone to perfect the concept and execute the cover design to the specs of the art department. Enter Sarah Brody on a white horse.

You are familiar with her work because she was the design force behind much of Apple's software applications. She photographed the Kawasaki Swallowtail, edited the picture, created the red gradient, chose the font (FFThesis-The Sans), laid out the cover, and generally made it perfect. This is the story of how I crowdsourced designs from

250 talented people around the world, selected one idea from an engineering student in Indonesia, convinced an origami master in Boston to create a new butterfly, and lucked out by knowing a designer in Silicon Valley. Can a story about a cover get more enchanting than this?

Colophon

Writing a book is an adventure. To begin with, it is a toy and an amusement. Then it becomes a mistress, then it becomes a master, then it becomes a tyrant. The last phase is that just as you are about to be reconciled to your servitude, you kill the monster, and fling him to the public.

—Sir Winston Churchill

Hardware: MacPro, MacBook Pro, iMac, iPad
Software: Microsoft Word, Firefox, TextExpander, iAnnotate, Dictionary
Websites: Twitter, TypePad, Quoteland, Quotations.com